TOWARDS FREEDOM

TOWARDS FREEDOM

A Journey of Discovery
through Rudolf Steiner's
Philosophy of Spiritual Activity

Evelyn Francis Capel

TEMPLE LODGE
London

Temple Lodge Publishing
51 Queen Caroline Street
London W6 9QL

Published by Temple Lodge 1993

A catalogue record for this book is available
from the British Library

ISBN 0 904693 53 8

Cover by S. Gulbekian

Typeset by DP Photosetting, Aylesbury, Bucks

Printed and bound in Great Britain by
Cromwell Press Limited, Broughton Gifford,
Wiltshire

*To the memory of Bert Capel
with loving thanks*

CONTENTS

PREFACE

The intention in this book is to follow the line of thought developed by the author of *The Philosophy of Spiritual Activity*, Rudolf Steiner, from the first chapter to the last. In style it will be like a journey into a strange country, in which one proceeds from question to question. Each of the chapters represents a stage on the journey and follows the same order as *The Philosophy of Spiritual Activity*. A commentary has been added to each chapter, with examples of how this adventure in thought is experienced in the world of today. It is hoped that the commentaries supplied will help people realize how their pilgrim's progress manifests itself today.

The examples quoted in *The Philosophy of Spiritual Activity* are all from the works of various philosophers. In the course of time, however, such philosophical ideas have been translated into psychologies. One can find examples of this in the behaviour and attitude of many people who do not study philosophy. It is therefore useful to say to oneself, in regard to the examples: whom have I met who thinks like that? Where are the influences left by the outlook of Kant in the minds of people who have never studied his work? In this manner one will discover that the inheritance of earlier ways of thinking reach into our own times. In contemplating the treasures of wisdom appearing in Steiner's book, one can understand that it is not really necessary to refer to an encyclopaedia, because if the reader considers carefully what is said he will find the problem related to that which he perceives in the psychological attitude of today. It will be more to the purpose to follow the questions raised in *The Philosophy of Spiritual Activity* and to take note of the examples known in one's own experience.

PART ONE

Knowledge of Freedom

Chapter 1

QUESTIONING

We live in a changing world and are changing ourselves. In remembering our own experiences, we know that there is more to come, but what this will be remains uncertain. This uncertainty prompts us to ask questions. Indeed, to do so, we must be willing to give up the quest for certainties. Our confidence must rest upon something different. Nowadays, all certainties are crumbling away. But what happens when we ask questions? Instead of drawing conclusions from previous experience or expectations, we face in wonder what is yet to come. Our whole mind makes a gesture of opening itself to what lies in the future. It is the phenomenon of the open mind in its true sense—the gesture of the mind willing to discover what it does not know, to give credit to new experience. If a conclusion is reached, the mind makes a gesture of shutting itself up and remaining satisfied with its conclusion. Hence, the adventure of new experience is over and the mind is at rest.

But our mental capacities can only be stretched when we realize that the world to which our questions are addressed is much bigger and more profound than we have previously understood. Further knowledge will only make itself known through further questioning and it will dawn on us that our certainties are in fact limitations. As more experience pours in, this becomes clearer. The following true story demonstrates this point. Some time ago, when cars had indicators to show which way they were going, a lady, who ought to have been a better driver than she was, encountered a policeman. He made no complaint but simply asked her a question, which was: how much horsepower has your car? Thrown into agitation, she replied that she thought it was 14. The policeman replied: 'Seven of your horses are going one way and seven the other.'

The shock of seeing her limitations as a driver so clearly had an effect on her which she never forgot.

Whereas it was the custom in Rudolf Steiner's lifetime for philosophers, in their books and their teaching, to bring forth conclusions, Rudolf Steiner made a new beginning by starting his first book on the subject from questions. The English title is *The Philosophy of Spiritual Activity*, in German *Die Philosophie der Freiheit*. The change in the form of the title was made at his request, for in English the difference between freedom and liberty has become obscure. It is wise to remember a historical fact that philosophy in the Middle Ages had developed through the custom of disputations. One thinker would set up a statement, which would then be discussed by everyone who wished to do so with regard to its reality. Philosophers often became travellers and were frequently from monasteries, where theological problems were discussed. Such a traveller would be given hospitality in another monastery when he had a proposition to set up and defend. As long as there was something to dispute and no conclusion had been reached, free hospitality was available to him. Should the disputation be concluded, the travelling philosopher moved on. At that stage in history, dispute was held to be the method of establishing truth, for to dispute was to activate the intellectual powers of the mind. A thinker could even dispute with himself; then he settled the matter privately. If he became a speaker with listeners, other people were involved. His disputation became a matter of teaching and instruction. By this method the intellectual powers of thinking minds were developed. But Rudolf Steiner belonged to a new age of history, an age which was just beginning. In technical terms it is often called the age of the consciousness soul.

That there are realities beyond those that a person has already grasped in his own mind is clear to everyone today. It is even possible to be discouraged into believing that one can never know what they are. In fact, more avenues are opened in the mind itself whenever a question is asked and faced. In the previous century, there was a French naturalist, Fabre, who had made many discoveries, especially in the area of insects. He was not happy with laboratories, where he found artificial circumstances. He preferred to look around his own neighbourhood in the South of France and to ask questions. He had a special ability never to forget the questions until they were answered.

Two trees stood outside his front door, which in summer were covered in cicadas making their singing noises from morning to night. At that time the scientific answer to the problem of sounds made by insects was that they were mating calls. This French naturalist considered the verdict and began to look along the branches of these trees. At long last he discovered that the males and females were always found perching next to each other. This observation provoked a large question in his·mind. How could the two be persistently calling to each other when they are always found side by side? Contemplating this problem, his power of imaginative thinking began to work and he began to believe that insects all over the Earth compose an orchestra which is heard in the world of the heavens. The song sounding on the Earth rises psalm-like into the universe, in response to the powers that create and maintain the wonders of nature in the world below.

Further and wonderful examples are to be found in Fabre's books of the creative value of asking questions. Returning to Rudolf Steiner's book on philosophy, the opening sentence is a question. It is addressed to the thinking and the action of the human being. Is he free in regard to what he thinks and does, or is he subject to a natural and unbreakable necessity? Steiner's book illustrates the many disputes that have already been made about such a question, some thinkers being in favour of freedom and others dismissing such an attitude as unscientific. What might be regarded as the greatest privilege of the human mind has often been treated as an illusion and, on the other hand, is defended by others as its most valuable gift. All matters of life, religion and science are involved with this question.

It is characteristic of *The Philosophy of Spiritual Activity* that examples are taken from classical writers on philosophy, some well known and some obscure. But life today shows that what was then philosophy has descended into the world of our everyday experience. We all meet these problems and can find them illustrated in our own affairs. Starting from conclusions quoted, especially in the first chapter, from acknowledged philosophers, we may find our own examples in what is around us which will appear more actual and important to ourselves. The experience offered by this book can become more valuable looked at from this point of view and made real in many studies in groups. One can say to oneself: when do I hear someone whose thinking is similar? When am I in danger of thinking like that myself? How is it possible to escape from this kind of problem?

Is freedom a matter of being able to make choices? That people today enjoy having many choices is demonstrated by the popular appeal of the supermarket, where the many items to choose from gives the impression of unlimited possibilities. But it does not solve the question of how the choice is made. The reason why some lines are more popular than others lies in the inner nature of the chooser. Forgotten memories, habits of taste, expectations of advantage all work together to persuade the customer that he is choosing. In reality he will be limiting himself to that which he already likes, or believes to be good for him. Where is the opportunity for freedom when the chooser is left out of the subject?

Herbert Spenser denied the reality of freedom, because he was sure that no one wanting, or not wanting, something, could decide the matter for himself. He was a victim of his own nature. Spinoza claimed that only God could be called free, because He exists out of the necessity of His own nature. If a stone is thrown, it continues to move in the direction in which it was set in motion. The stone will continue to fly along, believing that it is doing it out of its own intention. The baby cries for milk in the same manner, but other factors are present in the choice. Such examples cannot be compared with deliberate actions of conscience or heroism.

Two kinds of factors are to be considered (Eduard von Hartmann): those that work from outside, and those that work from within. How must the question of the freedom of the will be related to other questions? Is the matter different when there is a consciousness of making the decision? The distinction has to be made when it comes to actions of people, that a being who acts and a being who knows are both present. The one who can make decisions is the one who acts knowingly. It is therefore considered by some people that acting out of good sense is superior to acting out of animal instinct. But does good sense have a higher authority, or does it produce the same authority as hunger and thirst?

Hamerling believed that a human being can do what he intends, but he cannot intend out of his own will. But does one really believe this, although it is often found in real life. Taking action involves a reason and a motive. In this area there is still the question of free action. Where there is no control over the motive there can be no possibility of freedom. Clearly, where the law of the land is involved freedom is not possible. In other areas, for instance, where someone asks himself 'What will the neighbours say?' or 'Who is going to agree with me?', the motive often is not free. Every action is involved with a motive. Is my thinking involved? Then the decision to act arises in this form. The decision to act and thinking are involved with each other. It is useless to compare the instinctive actions of animals with those of human beings, who can think. Only actions which do not involve conscious motives can be compared with those of animals. An action cannot be free if the one who performs it does not know why he does so.

It has to be considered (Eduard von Hartmann) that two factors belong to a human action—that which belongs to the cause of the action on the one hand and the character of the one who is performing the action on the other. A situation may arise in which circumstances may determine the act. On the other hand, the character of the one who acts will also affect the carrying out of the action. For instance, a conversation once took place among some people with good intentions about the nature of hospitality. All were accustomed to receive invitations. The character of their upbringing caused them to feel that invitations should be returned. This went so far that in one family the principle involving 'a chop for a chop and a cutlet for a cutlet' prevailed. This procedure involved no impulse of freedom. Where was the person badly needing help to whom one would wish to give a cup of tea? Where were the generous impulses a kind person might feel to offer something that was not going to be returned? Could an act of hospitality be made outside the arrangement of conventional duties? It is clear that both inner and outer conditions would have to be transformed to produce a free action.

This presents a new question: what is the origin and meaning of thought? With such a question, one can appreciate the conclusion of the philosopher Hegel: 'Thinking makes the soul, which the animal also has, become spirit'. In this sense, thinking gives a special quality to human action. But can a person claim that all his actions are the result of deliberate thought? A distinction must be made between many kinds of action. Are there not intensive feelings connected with the problem? Does not the heart go to work with the head? Certainly this is so. But we can observe that the heart is approached through the head. The thought is the father of feeling. The more idealistic the thought-pictures about someone one loves, the stronger is the love. Those who cannot love have not been inspired with the necessary thoughts. Where one cannot understand the inspiration, only negative feelings are brought forth. The question of human action and its relation to freedom begins with thinking. A new question has to be faced: what is the nature of our capacity to think? The examples through which we have climbed, as one might climb over stiles on a walk, have brought us to a further view of what is at work in our capacity to *act*.

The question at the opening of this chapter has led the reader into a series of further questions that change the problem from the nature of action to who is performing it.

Through discovering the origin of an action in thinking, the mind passes from the action into awareness of the one who acts. It has taken the problem away from circumstances into the area of the human mind. Freedom is not a question of whether I can do what I want to do, or intend to do, or what my own intention is, but what my relationship is to the intention. How has it been formed? Freedom is a matter of inner relationships, which will have outer consequences.

We can see in this exploration a reflection of what has taken place in the evolution of mankind throughout history. The Law of Moses was a safeguard against the disintegration of human life on Earth. It does not speak of motives but of facts produced by actions. It forbids those actions that would ruin the conduct of human life. The motives underlying human action were taken up later by Jesus Christ, when He began His work on Earth with the thoughts in the Sermon on the Mount. The theme of the Sermon on the Mount is: it is not only a matter of what is done but of the inner intention in the soul of someone who acts, and its result.

Commentary

Looking back over the first chapter, recalling that the path of questioning has been traversed, what has happened now? We have discovered that the nature of freedom is not to be revealed in outer circumstances. I am not unfree when an influence from outside hinders me from realizing my intentions. The questions that freedom provoke are not in themselves addressed to circumstances; they begin with the consideration of what is going on within myself. I am the one who hinders the development of freedom from within, although I shall be likely to blame the world outside, unless I think carefully. If one watches the behaviour of small children in a supermarket, circumstances will seem to favour their opportunities for choice. On any shelf that a small child can reach, there will be a number of things he wishes to take home.

They are there and he can grab them. He is usually hindered from this action, especially if the father or mother is in charge of the shopping expedition. A great number of frustrated children will be encountered in the throes of the struggle to make them put down what they have picked up. Their nearest and dearest have come between them and their choice. After all, they will be paying the bill at the end, when the children are on the way home.

I was once asked to take a little boy to buy sweets. He was carrying the first purse containing coins that he had ever received, given him by a loving grandfather. We went, filled with joy, into a shop to face the many piles of sweets, knowing that we could buy as many as we pleased. A fine bag was handed over the counter to the boy. The purse was then requested from behind the counter. It was handed over in nice, plump condition, but it was returned thin and weak. The boy was shattered to see what had become of the wonderful purse. It was my business to explain that when the bag of sweets was fat, the purse would be the poorer. We returned to his home sadder and wiser. The choice of the sweets was fine, but the consequences were not. How was this?

It was the result of a choice made by himself. At this point, the reader may begin to sympathize with the philosopher Spinoza, who said that only God was free, because he could not be prevented from carrying out His intentions, whereas the human person would experience limitations. He chose a very strange example from the modern point of view—that of the stone in movement because it has been thrown. The stone is convinced that it moves out of its own energy, but it is in fact the object of a higher will, that of the person who throws. At that time in history, the difference between a thrown stone and an active person was not obvious.

If I run for a bus and it doesn't stop at my request, I make a discovery which extends the area of my consciousness and other questions arise. As in earlier days, it is still the custom to have stopping places for buses with notices reading 'Request stop'. The small child who wished to try this out would receive a cheery wave from the driver, but no stopping would take place. As a consequence, the child would ponder the problem of why his request was not answered. In so doing he or she learnt the differences between the child and the grown-up in the social customs of the age. When could the request be granted that was promised at the bus stop, and for whom? All grown-ups have developed their self-consciousness in encountering such situations. In this way they have realized that all human actions are not of the same type and are distinguished from each other by the phenomenon of consciousness. Freedom can have reality if it is sought in the inner process of the mind.

A later philosopher, von Hartmann, who lived in the nineteenth century, worked the matter out for himself. He found in his own being two forces that influenced how decisions are made from within. He noticed that a purpose for the action was present, but how it took place would depend upon the character and outlook of the human being involved with the action. What are the purposes which will inspire someone to an action? It is the business of advertising to make members of the public anxious to buy something. That in itself is quite simple, but other kinds of advertising have developed in modern times. Nowadays a large spade can appear as a picture on a hoarding. It carries different wording in different places, but one of the slogans is: 'This is the symbol of your personal energy to work and of private enterprise'. It is as if it would say: 'Your work depends on you, on what you carry within yourself as skill and energy, and the opportunities will be of your own making.' What is said of work is in fact what is said in this book about freedom: look first within yourself and find the human element from which the whole matter begins.

Looking into oneself, at one's humanity, is the beginning of a new path of questioning. Another philosopher (Hamerling) became convinced that people can do what they will, but they do not have control over the motives that release the will into action. Is the individual struggling to produce his own motives, or is he compelled by his own nature? In real life, people are often compelled by their own nature. They acquire longings and aims from outside. They want to be like others around them and therefore they listen to urges that are not really theirs. Those who want to escape into other circumstances do not often make those for themselves. They become tourists in large groups and are satisfied to do whatever everyone else does. They are afraid of what they would do out of their own initiative, and so lose their freedom. The question 'Dare I do what I choose myself?' prevents them from making their own decisions. But is this really necessary? Someone who is willing to look within himself to find the origin of his actions can also discover that he behaves differently, according to whether he is thinking for himself or taking his cue from the many opportunities in modern life to accept the thinking from outside. Have I taken my attitudes from the radio, television, the newspapers, the advice of neighbours, the advice of other people, or have I been willing to accept that I must stand on my own feet because my individual thinking lies within myself? From time to time a person should ask himself such a question. It would reveal the true nature of our ability to think.

It is easy today to confine thinking to oneself, to support one's personality with opinions that give me status in the world. But this is not the true meaning of thinking. It is the capacity that releases me from myself, because I can think beyond the limitations of character and circumstance and of all the influences that seek to tell me who I am. Thinking can carry me beyond myself into the mysteries of the universe, of mankind as a whole and the deeper meaning of history. Thinking can spread its wings, carrying me into the heights and the depths, into and beyond the area of my limitations. On its wings I can transcend my personality, the area of my selfishness, the hindrance to understanding. It gives me access to a larger world than myself, to which I really belong. Therefore, I can look to the philosopher Hegel, who believed that thinking raises me above my animal nature, above the limitations of earthly experience into the spiritual universe.

Chapter 2

THE SELF AND THE WORLD

Our ability to ask questions proves by experience to be a natural effect of our human constitution. If we, for example, look to the world of nature, we shall observe that it shows us effects, rousing in us a continual series of questions. We are familiar with what our senses show us about the world, but they provide us with experiences that raise more questions than they answer. When we look at a tree, we discover that its behaviour is continually changing. Sometimes the branches spread quietly over our heads; at other times they are restless and continually moving. Every variety of their behaviour makes us wonder why it takes place. Even our simplest observations cause us to be aware of the contrast between ourselves and the world. We are not at one with it, but are separate beings. This is made clear through the consciousness that arises in us, producing such questions. Beneath this level of consciousness, however, we have another kind of feeling which we never use, a feeling that we belong to the world of nature and are united with the whole universe.

We long to find the connection with the world that our consciousness seems to have broken. We are aware of an active spiritual life that seeks to link us with the larger reality. In religion, art and science, efforts are made to unite oneself with the world. Anyone who takes up clay modelling or painting is working with forms through which he finds himself while he is creating. Anyone who strives in thought to grasp the laws in the world is absorbing the content of the world into the content of his thought. In philosophical terms, the process of reconciliation will bring about a condition known as monism. If the thinker cannot transcend the consciousness that separates him from the world, he becomes a dualist and realizes that he is committed to the principle that such opposites as spirit and matter, subject and object, are the ultimate realities. But he discovers nevertheless that his constitution really connects him with both. If he becomes aware of the unity, he can overcome the split. The human mind can refuse to accept the spirit and become materialistic. It can deny the reality of matter and become spiritualistic, or it can assume that spirit and matter are naturally united to each other and are equally real.

Materialism can never produce a satisfactory explanation for the world, since every effort at an explanation must start with thinking, which is not a material process. Every materialistic argument leads to contradictions. Thoughts are not produced in the brain as the lower animal organs produce digestion. If the mind adopts mechanical processes in matter, the problem has simply been put somewhere else. Matter may appear to think for itself, but why should matter need to think *about* itself. A materialistic outlook does not solve the problem.

What happens if we start from the spiritualistic point of view, preferring to abandon the reality of matter? The ego experiences itself as a spiritual reality but if it cannot accept the reality of the sense world then it must remain shut up in itself. The famous philosopher Fichte attempted to work with this principle, with the result that he formed a false picture of the world, excluding all actual experience. In fact, neither materialism nor spiritualism can embrace all the facts. The opposite problem is experienced by the believing materialist. He includes in his thinking an activity which he believes comes from purely material processes, but he cannot be convinced that what his thinking produces is reality. There is, however, another solution, which is that matter and spirit are united naturally. But then comes the question: why does this take place in our experience? So often nowadays the answer is found in an act of faith instead of in wise thinking.

In this sense it becomes important to realize that the distinction between the material and the spiritual is the result of our own process of consciousness. A historical example of facing this problem is found in the works of Goethe, who said: 'Human beings are all in Nature and she is in all of them.' We are aware of having separated ourselves from nature, but we should realize that there is part of ourselves in which this is not so. We can only find nature outside ourselves when we have recognized its presence in our own being and constitution. When we ask questions of our experience of ourselves, we shall find that we are not only ourselves but more than that. We shall realize that in our daily experience we have to recognize forces of nature at work and must ask ourselves what they actually are.

Commentary

How do I experience my relationship to the world around me? It has seemed to me that the world in which I live provides me with many problems to solve and yet it is the only world I know. And this has been my fate for as long as I can remember. Once upon a time I was a small child who sat on a sandy shore and was quite convinced that the oncoming waves would swallow me up and that I must retreat from them. At the same time other little children round about rushed gladly into the waves and were tossed about until a grown-up came and pulled them out of the water. What does it mean that in infancy we already know two different ways of behaviour? In reality such behaviour does not depend on the world around but on something within oneself. When the self-consciousness is stronger, the fascination of the moving waves overcomes the nervousness of the self. The child can say: why should I not walk on the sea? It dreams one can do it, but in waking life it becomes dangerous and the child tends to say: where can I find help? The consciousness of oneself is the source of fear. What can I do with anything so powerful as the sea? If I sit on the bank and watch the wonderful movement, I am not afraid, but I wonder. If I am in the midst of the sea, my limitations appear and I realize that the waves are stronger than my limbs. All the sense impressions that arise from the body convince me that I must be afraid. But thoughts warn me that I must not stand back. I want to be one with the sea, but the evidence of my senses makes me afraid and I retreat within myself.

There is an old fairy-story called 'The Prince who was Afraid of Nothing'. Its theme is the importance of the prince learning to be afraid. Why should this be so? The prince, who is the human soul, has no correct relationship with the world if he does not know fear, because then he does not know himself. As fear makes one realize the difference between oneself and the world, so courage can only come from extending consciousness beyond this point. Nevertheless, there are many experiences that remind us that we are not separated from the world but are at one with it. In thirst one knows the value of finding water to quench it. But where is the water? It descends in the rain from the clouds, it rises up through a spring or a fountain and is easily caught for a good drink. And yet the sea itself causes thirst and does not provide drink: 'Water, water everywhere and not a drop to drink'.* The human soul constantly moves between the memory of being at one with the world and the irritation of being roused to self-awareness through the experience of being separated from the world. And so it comes about that the first step on the path of discovery through questions leads the traveller through the problem of why he experiences separation from the world and receives self-awareness. But how can he find the world again?

I can think and discover myself in separation. The world shows me its material nature; my ability to think reveals its spiritual nature. Am I therefore obliged to know myself as spirit and accept the world around me as material? If my ability to think is extended so that I can find what is spiritual in the world around, the barrier produced by myself is overcome. I can likewise think the world in its spiritual nature. When does the rose bush reveal itself to me? The answer must

* *The Rime of the Ancient Mariner* by Samuel Taylor Coleridge.

be that as long as I can think through the changing processes that take place in the course of the seasons I can grasp that the process of growth, the showing of leaves and blossoming are the true revelation of what lives as spirit in the bush. Altogether they show what moves as spirit over the rose bush. If you wish to present the rose itself to another person, are you going to hand him a bare branch, a bud, or a full-blown rose about to fade? The parts are not the whole, only that which lives within one's thought when the spiritual process is comprehended. Then I have joined my personal awareness to that which the rose is proclaiming to the world. There was once a rose grower who would never allow two blossoms to be put into the same vase, because he saw each one complete in itself.

Such thinking allows my self to find itself within the world again. But if thinking is omitted, the world remains material and separated. In contrast, there is also the way of thinking that refuses to recognize the reality of the material world. Both can be brought together in thought, allowing a modern person to believe that in the original being of the atom matter and spirit are united, but this notion only takes the question and puts it in another place. It has taken the imaginative thinking of someone like Goethe to realize that, in spite of our self-consciousness, we are all one with with Nature and so united with her. We easily recognize this when we experience our bodily condition reflecting in ourselves actual processes. It is a strange fact that bodily pain belongs to the impact of the world around upon our human nature, but pain is experienced very differently by different people according to their constitution. Everyone who has tried warning another person that he is going to experience pain discovers that what is painful to him can produce quite different reactions in others. The outer facts have varying effects upon the consciousness of different people. But when we encounter the working of natural causes in our own constitution, we find that the different constitution is in itself produced by its ability to unite itself with nature— though in different degrees. It is necessary to recognize the fact that my constitution lives in a whole world of natural processes, but they are diversified by my own being with its individual consciousness. We live in nature, but each one in his own unique way.

Chapter 3

THINKING

Within the adventure of asking questions and yet more questions, we now move on to consider when we find ourselves thinking and what it really is. Considering it in terms of exploring spiritual activity, the example offered in *The Philosophy of Spiritual Activity* is illustrated by the game of billiards. Nowadays, there is a popular version of the game called snooker, so that an example which for a long time was old-fashioned is now up to date. Anyone who wants to know more about the example can easily find access to a game of snooker, in which he can set up for himself the experience described in chapter 3 of *The Philosophy of Spiritual Activity*. He can observe the movement of the ball, and can observe the effect of the first ball on the second one. All this can be observed as something happening without his own influence, but, if the observer begins to form thoughts about what he sees, he finds himself involved in what depends on himself. The thoughtful observer is aware of a double activity. He observes what is taking place outside himself; he also discovers that the thinking with which he explains to himself what is going on is his own activity.

He has become aware of a twofold experience: that which is taking place outside himself and that which he can produce out of himself. Observing and thinking make up his experience. In our ordinary affairs the two tend to become confused, but in the game of snooker they are clearly defined. I observe and add to what I see my capacity to think. Without my activity, I would not be able to observe what especially belongs to me, thinking. It is the active part of me in the situation that I have to exercise in order to observe it. What do I gain by it? Observing will throw up a series of separate experiences. If their relationship to each other is to be experienced, thinking is necessary. If I follow the position of the ball on the table and watch its changes, I am looking on. When I begin to understand the processes that I am observing, they begin to make sense. I am still an onlooker, but understanding and purpose begin to reveal themselves to me through my own inner activity. I become aware of myself watching what is going on, but this activity makes sense of what I observe. In becoming an active part of the world, do I therefore not belong to it? Am I absorbed in this experience: here am I and there is the rest of the world?

In reality I brought about this situation myself by thinking and observing. My capacity to think introduces me to a twofold relationship. I can both observe and think. The origin of my situation does not lie in the world itself; it lies within me. Once I have begun to think, and at the same time to observe, I find that in the twofoldness of my capacity lies the double activity producing the impression that the world and I are separated. But this is not really so. I may believe that everything I experience around me and observe is the world. But by thinking I add to my observations that part of the world which I have made myself. However, I do not add to my observations that part of the world which I have produced through my own effort until I have finished thinking. Thinking has to be achieved before I can observe it. Because I have produced thought by means of my own activity, I cannot observe it until it is done. It is there and I must look back on it.

But something has taken place. To the finished world around me which I can observe, a new element has been added, produced by myself. I am not simply an onlooker—I am aware of creating something. Although I can only see it by looking back, it is the one reality of which I can be sure. I know how it has come about, because I have made it myself. But my activity of creating is all-absorbing. I cannot observe what I have done until I look back. If I stand at the edge of a great stream of traffic wondering when I dare to cross the road, it seems to me that here I am facing the world. But the situation has been brought about by myself from the moment when I discovered myself thinking. I have been created at one with the world and I can establish this when I observe that within me which belongs to the world. When I discover what is really of myself, because I have produced it, then I can see the relation between what I find within myself and what I observe. No one but myself has brought about the sense of separation. But how could I be a responsible person without that recognizable experience?

In the act of thinking we have found the core of what is taking place. In all that I observe without thinking, I am involved but I do not know how the situation comes about. Therefore, in the questions put to me by the world, the main consideration must always be the contemplation of thinking. I cannot claim that the picture made by thinking in another intelligence is truer than my own. I am a thinking being. The faculty belongs to me. Therefore I am aware that in my consideration of the world I must begin with thinking. It is a principle that bears witness to itself. In order to go behind the thoughts of the activity that produces them, we must ask yet another question. We have spoken of thinking without describing what carries it, that is to say, the human consciousness. Should we start from this point, or from thinking itself? They depend upon each other, but if I wish to know how they are related I will have to start with thinking. If someone wishes to understand consciousness, he must begin by observing thinking. This would be a problem if the philosopher were creating the world, but actually he is understanding it. Thinking is a reality for itself, regardless of subject or object, for then we have concepts that have already been brought about by thinking. This must be the starting point. Man is not the beginning of creation, but the end. Therefore, to explain the world, he must begin with that which he finds nearest to hand. We cannot go back to what we believe is the beginning, so we must begin with that which is most clear to us. That which has developed in man and is now at his service is thinking. Thinking is a fact. Whether it is right or wrong is not the point. It is the instrument that I have at my disposal to grasp the world. It may be possible to wonder if it is being rightly used, but that it is there cannot be doubted.

It has been assumed in this discussion that thinking is a different activity of the soul from any other and that this can be observed. There is no other activity of the soul dependent upon my ego. One must distinguish between having thought pictures and thinking. One must observe that nothing belongs to the reality of thinking that is not to be found within thinking.

In this chapter the reader is not dealing with thoughts that may be right or wrong; he is looking at thinking as an activity which would not be there without our human selves. In the many news items that reach us in the course of a day, it would seem as if reality lay with action and that thinking produced a commentary on what should, or should not, be happening, excluding us from any participation. If we can see how thinking plays a real part in the situation we hear of, then our responsibility develops through what we know. The world with its diverse peoples living in other circumstances would then live in us as part of ourselves. In this hard world of today it is a temptation to wish to be released from the trials of knowing. The real point is, however, that in active thinking we are participating.

Commentary

On the journey along the path of questioning, the situation arises at this stage in the book that one's own ability to think is directly experienced. In order to take this step, however, a lot of very common illusions have to be overcome. One illusion is that thinking is a part of myself that provides me with my opinions. Working through the examples in this chapter, this illusion is overcome when one notices one's own thinking as it really is. There are many occasions when someone feels the need to assert himself, with the help of opinions and a point of view which they seek to uphold. Nowadays this is frequently an experience. Thinking provides me with a viewpoint. It allows me, within a democratic outlook, to claim the right to my own opinion. If I go to vote in an election, I take this right with me, establishing myself as a person with a name and address and the claims of a citizen. Other people with quite different opinions will be able to claim the same right. It leads us into the social situation in which power rests with the majority. But how often does greater wisdom show itself in the majority? If the subsequent government makes serious errors, the majority reaps the reward of its own illusions. The government can be blamed, but it has been put in power by the opinions of the majority with the right to vote.

Social occasions, as can be experienced in every pub, depend on arguments over points of view. Once again thinking provides weapons for discussion. Mostly, these battles of wit do not bring much contact with reality, but each competitor is establishing his identity through his opinion. Nowadays, arguments can deteriorate into a kind of sport, each game won by those who can dispute most effectively. But the example provided at the beginning of this chapter (in *The Philosophy of Spiritual Activity*) does not lead to opinion, but to fact. When I can no longer see the ball in the game of snooker and it continues in my thinking, no matter of opinion is taken into account but only what in fact happens to the ball. My thinking is included in the action and the result is that it becomes connected with the facts of the game, truly or untruly. Such an example lifts thinking out of the area of personal opinions into the facts beyond me and in the world itself.

There are many factors in the experiences of every day which make me an onlooker in a world of activity beyond myself. What has to be discovered along this path of thought is that this is not so, unless I am pushed into it by experience. Frequently, the modern person is made into an onlooker by circumstances. In the world of sport a game is played in front of onlookers. A few people play the game and many look on, expressing their opinions. Through radio and television, a commentator leads the way. He does not play the game himself, but he is willing to tell the world where mistakes have been made, where illusions have been at work. But he does nothing himself, except produce opinions. Everyone can have opinions, but they do not affect what is actually done by the players. The position of the onlooker is pleasant. It does not matter if his opinion is right or wrong. He is saved from every consequence by his position in the gallery. Having taken refuge in onlooking, he becomes at ease, while the burden of real action is borne by the players. It is no wonder that a leading newspaper could recently carry an article describing how weak the players in the match had become and how strong and critical were the onlookers. In reality, the situation is based on misunderstanding.

Thinking is my inner capacity that allows me to become active in the world beyond my consciousness of myself. A person of today feels himself to be shut up within his personality. But every time he thinks beyond the range of opinion he is drawn into the larger world outside himself and becomes active in it, because his thinking can enter the objective world and allow him to partake in it. Should he return to the world within and to his own point of view, he will do this through the inner capacity of feeling; but in the activity of thinking he emerges into the world itself with a strength of understanding. At this stage of the journey through questioning, a person emerges from his personality and enters the world itself through the ability to think. He ceases to be an onlooker by adding to the reality of the world through the grasp of ideas.

He encounters the world around him by observing what he apprehends. When thinking is added to observing, the mind takes part in what is happening in the activity of knowing. When this activity is expressed in language, it can be described by saying that through the activity of observation the mind grasps the percept. When this is united with the concept, or thought, then the thinking person knows. He becomes aware of himself, taking a real part in the world in which he lives, through adding the concept produced by the inner activity of thinking to what his senses perceive. In uniting the two, he becomes the bearer of the idea. The ability to observe does not produce the thought. It provides impressions, one after the other, that make sense by means of the inner activity of producing ideas. The human mind knows by means of the process of uniting what comes through observation with what comes from the opposite direction, through producing thoughts. The effect of combining the two is knowing, and the person who knows is myself. Each person produces the activity out of himself, but all share the world which is known. Varying impressions can be produced, depending on the abilities of individual people. But the process is shared by everyone and can give rise to unity, without depriving anyone of his separate identity.

We are not world creators, but we know the world and encounter a reality greater than our personality by means of the activity that can be produced in us through the objective nature of thinking. Here is an example. Let us imagine a group of people looking at a tree. Individually they may observe differently, according to where they are standing and to the capacity of the senses with which they observe. Their observation, however, unites them in the idea of the tree, which all can grasp with their ability to think. They are bringing to the tree itself, which lies outside them, the idea that belongs to it and which has been separated by the way in which the tree has become physical reality available to the senses. But we can all bring the idea of the tree to it as it stands with branch, bark, colour and shape before us. In the ability of his inner life to unite observation and thought, man is made part of the world in which he is living. He is also made aware that his thinking belongs to himself and, if it is exercised to the full, unites him with what is real. The person who exercises his mind ceases to be an onlooker. He can think for himself and develop the ability to do so, whereby he faces reality. In the act of self-discovery, the individual person knows himself to be a real part of the processes in the world. He seeks beyond himself true ideas and, in so doing, outstrips his personality and becomes a true self, beyond opinion. On this path of discovery through question, which leads to further questions, the human mind becomes able to see himself as a real being in a real world and so can transcend himself through his own inner activity.

Chapter 4

PERCEPTIONS

Concepts and ideas are the result of thinking. When observing, the thinker seems to produce pictures that belong to the concept. The concept remains behind when the thing perceived disappears, and so the more we experience the greater will be our range of concepts. But no concept stands alone—it is taken up into a collection of concepts. For instance, the single concept of a lion becomes part of the whole concept of lions as such. Ideas are of the same quality as concepts. They are the result of thinking and its consequence. But the concept cannot be extracted from the observation itself; in fact, the human being gradually adds concepts to the objects of observation. An example is taken from Herbert Spencer. He believed that he went through a wood in September, heard a noise and watched the grass moving. He found a pheasant in a ditch and was satisfied that he had found the cause of what was happening. But his mental process is not sufficiently explained. Hearing a sound causes me to look for a concept related to the observation. The concept carries me beyond the sound. Further thinking makes clear to me that the sound is the effect of a cause. Only when I have combined the concept with the observation can I seek further for the cause. I shall never find the concept of cause and effect without thinking. Observing arouses thinking and leads me to thought.

Now it is useful to pass from thinking to the being who thinks. In this way, thinking is connected with observing. Concepts and percepts meet in the area of human consciousness. As a person observes an object, it is a given part of his world. But when he thinks, he realizes that this activity has been brought about by himself. He then tends to regard the thing observed as object and himself as the thinking subject.

He achieves self-consciousness. When he is aware of his own activity he becomes the subject, and what he has observed becomes the object. But this process of thinking makes oneself the subject, while what is thought about becomes the object. And it is only through thinking that he arrives at the experience of subject and object. Thinking is not subjective, because it has led him to the experience of the activity of thinking, which is beyond subject and object. The subject only becomes the object through the power of thinking. A person's sense of individuality is the gift of his thinking. The double nature of man is revealed, for, in thinking, he connects himself to the rest of the world. But he also experiences himself, through thinking, as an individual.

A new question arises. How does it come about that the other element—the object of observation—unites with thinking in consciousness? Here we are in trouble, because we would have to separate all that comes through thinking in the sphere of our observation. But the content of our consciousness is already filled with concepts. Can I imagine a being with human intelligence arising out of nothing and confronting the world? He would perceive the content of observation alone and would notice only a collection of objects of perception—for instance, impressions of colour, warmth, taste, smell and liking and disliking. Such is the quality of observation alone. Experience shows that thinking can bring together different elements from observation and relate them to each other. As the activity of thinking is not subjective, the relationships brought about by thinking are not subjective either. Therefore, we have to seek in our thinking activity the effect on our conscious subject. What is there for me as a conscious subject that should now be called percepts which meet the concepts through thinking? We can also call what originally appears in our thinking consciousness a percept. The naive person regards his percepts as things that have an existence separate from himself. In observing a tree, he does so in this style; if he observes again, he accepts this as a separate observation. An example is the small child trying to put his hand on the Moon.

Every percept obliges us to make another to go along with it. Why are we continually obliged to rectify our observations by making others? If I stand at one end of an avenue of trees, those in the distance appear smaller. If I go to the other end, my experience is reversed. All our percepts are influenced by the place where we are standing when we have them. But they are also dependent on our physical and spiritual constitution at the time.

Our constitution affects our ability to observe. Colour blind people, for example, only see differences of shade between bright and dark. Therefore one has to decide whether one's impressions gained through observation are subjective. We can even begin to wonder if our observations have any objective value. The most famous thinker on this problem was George Berkeley. He maintained that there is no evidence, beyond that of one's own spirit, that anything that exists is there outside one's own consciousness. There is no colour without an eye that sees it. There is no sound without an ear that hears. There is no world, apart from my perception of it. What we perceive as an object is only a connection of observations. This provides us with a difficult question. If I leave my bedroom and go downstairs, what evidence have I that the bed is still there, except when I return to see it? Sending someone else to look is no help, because so long as he looks, the bed will be there.

Bishop Berkeley's own view of this matter is expressed in one of his sayings: 'All the choir of Heaven and furniture of Earth—in a word all those bodies which compose the mighty frame of the world—have not any substance without a mind.' But another question arises: what is the function of our ability to observe? The answer lies in turning from the object of the perception to the subject. I also perceive myself. That shows me that I am the constant element, compared with the coming and going of pictures and observations. Within my consciousness, the perception of myself occurs while I have other perceptions. I continue, not only to be conscious of the object, but of my own personality. I see a tree and know that I am

seeing it. In the process I have acquired something else. I am
aware of mental pictures. I observe them in the mental picture
of myself. What I have observed changes my inner life and I
can speak of mental pictures. While other observations come
to me from outside, from within I have the observation of
myself. This raises the further question of whether I experience
anything but the effects of objects that I am no longer looking
at. It has been claimed that we only live in the mental pictures
left behind in our minds.

Comparing this opinion with Bishop Berkeley's one finds
that it is not the same, because Berkeley believed that my
observations come about through the power of God. I do not
see a table, because God provides me with the percept of the
table. Kant's view of the matter is different. Whereas Berkeley
maintained that nothing exists outside our observations,
Kant, on the contrary, states that only our consciousness
shows us what occurs and that we cannot know what is taking
place in the thing itself. We can only know our mental pictures
and can rely upon nothing else. But they depend upon the
organization of our inner being. They are therefore affected by
them, so that for us knowledge and the mental picture are the
same thing. What I experience through the senses is due to the
fact that I am outside the body and only experience the effects
of its influence on my organization.

It is believed that our senses can only transmit to us what
comes from themselves, and not from that which comes from
the world outside. The naive person believes that the objects as
he perceives them exist outside his consciousness. But the
scientific view is that our perceptions result from the mod-
ifications of our own organism. For instance, consider the eye
and the ear, both complicated organs. From the end of the
nerves a stimulation is passed along to the brain, so that a
number of processes have taken place before their effect
becomes conscious. What the brain tells the soul is therefore
regarded as either the effect of outer processes or of what
happens within the brain. What we have in our consciousness,
however, are not processes in the brain, but impressions. My

impression of the colour red is not the same as the processes
that take place in the brain. In the last resort, my soul only
knows what has been brought about by a process in the brain.
It takes hold of these impressions and transforms them into
experiences of the body. The brain tells me about the different
kinds of impression made on me. For instance, the mental
picture of the trumpet's call is the final result of the impression
made on my senses. On its way to the soul via the brain the
outer fact is completely lost.

Commentary

This way of thinking has produced, in the times following the
writing of *The Philosophy of Spiritual Activity*, certain historical attitudes and problems. For instance, how many people are there today who think of the world and themselves in
terms of what they would like it to be? If one believes that the
realities are outside the realm of our consciousness, if the thing
itself is always hidden, a certain kind of irresponsibility can set
in. If the truth is far away from us, we can start to mould our
human world in terms of our wishes and aspirations. Nowadays, great confusion has arisen about the nature and man-
agement of wealth. Is the money we have in the bank a reality
that will last all our lifetime? What about the great fraudsters
who have been dealing with the money that we believed was an
investment for our future? Who is going to believe for long
that modern inventions are doing no harm to nature? What
effect will the contamination of the air have on us? We oscil-
late between the carefree use of resources and the panic that
arises when harmful effects start to show. Such experiences
have followed the optimism that attended the introduction of
so many of our modern great inventions.
    Not long ago a fearsome advertisement was shown with a
picture of three party political leaders. Each of them was
supposed to be saying: 'This is my party, I can tell what lies I
like.' Such an attitude comes about by extending into practical

life the attitude of mind which began with the philosophers who said: 'The world is my representation. I am cut off from the thing itself.' Why in such an unreal world can I not bring about what I wish for? As it's not the real world, why shouldn't I have it all my own way? This was once a philosophy, of which the danger was not seen. It has now been translated into action, with manifold deeds of immorality.

The naive attitude towards perceived things is that thinking would not be there if we had no senses. No eye, no colour. The eye enters into an exchange with the object. There is no chemical process involved, because that only takes place in the nerve going to the brain. The colour is produced by the soul, which then attaches it to a body outside—and that is what I believe to have perceived. I must then accept that my soul has produced what, if I am naive enough, I believe to exist outside.

Now I must recognize that this modification in my soul condition disappears with my mental picture. I would have no right to speak of the real eye but only of my mental picture of the eye. If I continue in this vein, I would have to reckon in a similar way with other percepts, all of which come from the percept of my organism. But I would then have to acknowledge that the way to external observation ends with a process within my own brain, and one moreover which I cannot perceive. On the way from the process in the brain to the impression, the process of observation is broken. There is no logic in the way that the impression and the mental picture are related to each other. Two areas of observation have been confused and no reconciliation can be found. If one treats one's objective organization as belonging only to a complex that can be translated into a mental picture, the process stops. One cannot also accept the principle that the world which I perceive is my mental picture, as was maintained by Schopenhauer. It would have to be accepted that one knows neither the Sun nor the Earth, but only an eye that sees the Sun and a hand that can feel the Earth. One must accept that the eye and the hand are no less perceptions than the Sun or the Earth.

They are just as much mental pictures. Then, gradually, everything about me becomes a modification.

It is natural to believe that, if my actions do not touch a real world but only one based on impressions, I can substitute wishes for facts. But such an attitude injures my respect for truth. I become a shadow of myself. If Kant is right and I do not deal with the thing itself, but only with its representation, then I am hidden from myself. I can feel myself exposed to hidden realities and my life of thought becomes a collection of theories. They appear attractive if they arise from representations that turn into assumptions. The following story told during wartime, about mothers who collected cereals reserved for babies from the Health Centre, is a useful example. One day, ants invaded the stock in the Health Centre. The staff who distributed it were worried about the wrath of the mothers, so they simply enquired if what they had handed out suited the babies. The mothers replied that they were happy about the distribution, because when they got home they could see the vitamin B running about in it. These were of course the ants, but the impression produced by what they had been told was so strong that they were happy to have it confirmed! They were encountering what their impressions had allowed them to expect.

What one can easily imagine becomes in the present time what the mind is willing to accept. But no sense of responsibility can be cultivated in this manner. Clever frauds have been uncovered in financial systems that people have always regarded as safe. These frauds have been discovered after they have been going on for quite a long time. They are the direct result of living with thoughts unconnected with facts. But the human mind has the capacity to find reality through thinking, although this has been denied by the powerful influence of such prophets as Kant. It is in the realm of fact that wishes reveal themselves for what they are. Things like vitamins and germs, for example, are not available to our observation. We represent them to ourselves as though we would expect to observe them frequently. They are theories which we use as explanations because we imagine them to be observable. A fellow traveller in a railway carriage once demanded that the window be opened to let in the cold wind, because she announced that the carriage was full of germs. Everyone present accepted her right to talk in that way. And yet, she was simply using an assumption that could be imagined. Where can we find the facts?

If a person reflects on what has reached him through observation, he will discover that another reality meets him in the concept. This reality is never attained merely by observation, but by the union between what is conceived and what is perceived. The concept is based on what is real in the spiritual world and the percept on what is real in the physical world. If, for instance, one observes a tree that one knows to be an oak, the concept of the oak comes about through thinking. The concept has its real origin in the cosmos and the details of what one can observe are revealed through the senses of sight, touch and smell, which acquire their meaning through the concept. The tree has developed physically into a fact of the sense world, but the other part of the reality comes to meet it through the ability of the observer to think what the cosmic pattern of the oak is in the higher world. This is a fact of existence that can be realized if the mind does not hurry over the process by the assumption 'I have seen it and so it must be an oak tree'.

Can there be errors in the way that concept and percept are brought together? There can be, and they will be experienced in the following way. In childhood one can notice that the mental picture often clashes with the sense observation. I can recall as a child having a magnificent picture in my mind of the lion, which was not to be seen in my ordinary surroundings. When I was taken by a kindly relative to a zoo, my chief impression was one of disappointment when I actually saw the animal. I was too polite to complain to the relative, but to myself I said: 'I know more in my own mind about the reality of the lion than the unhappy creature I have seen in the cage.'

A further experience can arise when strange and unknown

percepts are suddenly encountered and the concept has to be sought consciously. The following example is taken from modern aerial warfare. Through the ingenious inventions that are possible nowadays, errors can be brought about in the realm of mental pictures. In order to bear unknown danger bravely, people tend to adopt new mental pictures and give them names. In World War II, when new weapons of mass destruction were constantly being invented, the British people had not only to deal with terrifying new experiences but to find names which allowed these experiences to be met with courage and common sense. The pilotless enemy aircraft which started to cross the Channel were so constructed that, when their propulsive power cut out, they came down and exploded. One day a kind of pet name for them was hit on, and they were called 'Doodle Bugs'. From then on they were treated as unpleasant but familiar objects. Panic evaporated and everyone began to feel like the little boy who said in his evening prayers: 'Please God, give the Doodle Bugs strength to carry on.' When concepts and percepts are constructed from reality, the human mind grasps this reality and can therefore develop a sense of responsibility.

Chapter 5

THE ACT OF KNOWING

How is the relationship between percepts and mental pictures formed? If one follows what the naive realist assumes about the constitution of the individual, then we do not encounter the things themselves but only their mental pictures. But one must consider the problem of the critical idealist, who assumes that the world is his mental picture and has no confirmation for his concept. It is one thing to ask if this line of thought is correct, and another to consider the value of the proofs. In fact they have no value. The problem can be expressed in a picture. If a house is being built and, in erecting the first floor, the ground floor falls apart, then the first floor breaks down too.

If the perceived world is only part of my mental picture and its effect upon me comes from that which cannot be perceived, then our mental pictures depend upon that which is outside our consciousness. How can we know anything about something which is not accessible to our observation? If the thinker is concerned about the connection between his conscious percepts and the unconscious causes, the percepts disappear as he turns his attention away from the things themselves. If one imagines that the things one sees are only reflections, then one can find only an indirect connection with what is there. The so-called critical idealist can say: I am shut up in the world of my mental pictures and cannot get out. When I think about the thing which is behind my mental pictures, then this is also a mental picture. Such an idealist must refute the thing itself and say: it has no meaning because it is not there. Such a person sees the whole world as a dream. There are only two kinds of people: those who live with their dream pictures as if they were real things, and those who recognize the unreality of the dream world, but whose own personality is a dream. He who refuses to see that there are things of which we have no knowledge must say the same of his own personality. All reality becomes a wonderful dream, in which there is no spirit that dreams. The philosopher Fichte recognized this difficulty. In this form of experience there can be no confidence in science. Either all is illusion, or there is a higher kind of realism called transcendental. Both points of view arise from research into perceptions.

How then does the ego produce its world of pictures? Supposing that our experiences were all mental pictures and our daily life a dream, then knowledge would be the act of waking up. The pictures in our dreams are only interesting so long as we are dreaming. When we wake up, we have questions about the processes that brought them about and want to know why we must follow certain dream pictures. If I dream that I am drinking wine, when I wake up it doesn't interest me at all. But observation shows that the experience of dreaming is in contrast to what we find when we wake up. In fact, however, we have a condition where the state of wakefulness itself encounters dreaming. It does this in thinking. If we overcome a naive state of mind, another question arises: what is the relationship between thinking and perceiving? Whatever the nature of my percept, I can only say something about it with the help of thinking. If I say that the world is my representation, that is itself the result of thinking. It is important to realize that, in our inner activity, thinking is often overlooked. This comes about because, in thinking about an object, we concentrate upon it rather than on the experience of thinking. The world is regarded as finished in itself and the thought picture which a person makes is in his own head. The world is complete without it. But another question arises: with what right does one insist that the world is complete without thought? Does not the world charm forth thinking out of the human mind in the same way that blossoms are brought forth in plants? Why should thoughts not have the same natural relationships to thinking that leaves and blossoms have to plants? Just as blossoms and leaves only appear on the plant when their seeds have been sown in the earth and exposed to light and air, so the concept of the plant can only appear when it is contacted by a thinking consciousness.

It is quite illogical to believe our perception of something is the totality and what comes about through thinking is something added to it which does not belong to it. A rosebud isn't merely what I observe, for when I put it in water it will gradually blossom and be something different. What I observe at one moment is not the whole. It is equally wrong to regard the whole sum of what can be observed as a thing itself. Take another example. If I throw a stone through the air in a horizontal direction, I see it in different places one after the other. I combine them in thought to produce a mathematical form. If I follow the course that the stone takes, it takes the same form. It is an essential part of the whole process of the stone being thrown. If I had only a series of visual perceptions, I would not discover the form within the appearance. This is provided by thinking. The whole process does not reveal itself as a unity, because our consciousness only allows us to perceive from two directions at once: perceiving and thinking.

It has nothing to do with the nature of the things themselves that the human being is organized to be aware of them in this form. He is limited. On the one hand, he is a being among other beings; his existence belongs to space and time, so that he can only experience the universe in bits and pieces. If this were otherwise, the whole universe would appear to him at once and there would be no distinction between himself and other things. The cosmos would be a unity and a whole. There would be no break in the course of events. But it has become a necessity for our human consciousness to deal with special qualities separately if we are to become aware of them. Our eyes can see separate colours, one after the other; our comprehension can grasp concepts, one after the other. But this ability to break up the whole is a subjective concern, because it makes clear to us that we are not identical with the world process as a whole but as one being among others.

Our relationship to other beings should be made clear. Observation shows me the sum of characteristics which I gather together into my personality in the same way that I observe the characteristics of a metal and realize it to be gold. The same thing is done through thinking about myself. Self-observation leaves me with a particular picture: thinking takes me right beyond these limits. I am, in fact, a double being. I am limited in so far as I observe my personality, but within me I bear an activity which invades my limited existence from a higher sphere. Our thinking is not as individual as our feeling and sensitivity are. It is universal. It is individualized in each person, because it encounters individual feeling and sensitivity. The particular form that universal thinking shows in different people separates them. But a triangle is the same concept for everyone, even if it is imagined individually. Prejudice has to be overcome here. A person does not form his own concepts, which belong to him; everyone has a common concept of a triangle. In this sense, thinking is a common possession. In thinking we meet the element binding individualities with the cosmos. We are separated in our sensitive feelings but, when we think, we belong to one universal Being. That is the deeper reason for our double nature. We can experience a universal force coming into being, not streaming from the centre of the world but from each point on the periphery. We know our own existence within certain limits, but we learn to understand what is beyond our own being with the help of the thinking that streams into us.

Because our thinking reaches beyond our separate existence towards the whole, we have within us the striving for knowledge. Beings who cannot think do not have this urge. The act of knowledge is the synthesis of percept and concept; they are the reality of the thing itself. It is a waste of time to ask oneself whether there is another way of overcoming the separation in the world, except through the content of the idea which is given us by thinking. One can believe that a human personal god may do this, or the will without thought, as Schopenhauer suggested. They both belong to the limited area of our observation, for the will is only the activity of our personality. Schopenhauer rejected thinking as being the bearer of world unity, because he wanted that which seemed to him completely real. For him, the body was identical with the individual, in one sense as an object among objects and, in another, as activity identified with the word 'will'. Each act of will depends upon movements of the body. The will appeared to him to show itself in two ways: through comprehension and understanding, and through the body of the human being, when actions appeared as a directly observable reality. He overlooked the fact that observation of oneself is not different from other observations and depends upon bringing together concepts and ideas. Anyone who believes that thinking is entirely abstract has failed to realize what perceiving without the concept actually is. Thinking weaves its threads from being to being and gives it content. Only in this way can I understand the world around me, even to the point of contrast, such as that between the snail and the lion. So the content of the world of ideas comes to meet the human being. The content of perception is revealed from outside, the thought content from within. This may be called intuition. Observation and intuition are the sources of our knowledge. If the ability to find the intuitions that belong to things is missing, then there is no true content to the world. To explain something and make it understandable means putting it into the connection to which it belongs, from which human consciousness had separated it. This is what human mental activity does—it separates into above and below, before and after, cause and effect, object and subject. Therefore our own intuitions connect what is separated into a unified world, which we have ourselves broken up through the twin activities of thinking and perceiving.

A further question is: when is it recognized that thinking has an absolute authority? For example, take the colour red. It enters my consciousness. In experience it is always connected with other percepts, with other objects belonging to the sense world. Other realities appear in the same setting. I can continue to look at processes in which other objects are revealed to my sense organs; these turn out to have no connection with the original perceptions. The same thing happens when I look for further connections between the sense organs and the brain. I continue to have new percepts. But what unites these separate experiences? Only thinking does this. One can imagine that no colour is present without an eye sensitive to colours, but this will only be true if the observation is connected with thinking. So the further question arises: what is perception? There is no answer, except to realize that it is given meaning by the reality of the intuition belonging to it. I can remain aware of an object of perception even when it is no longer within my sphere of observation. I can have a picture of a table, for example, after the table has disappeared from sight. I am able to have a mental picture of the table because, through its presence, it has altered what has happened in the field of my vision. The mental picture is a subjective perception in contrast to the objective perception when the object is present. This can confuse the mind about the nature of perception. In practice we can observe the relationship between the mental picture and the object, thus revealing the frontier between the human subject and the external object.

Anyone who asks himself questions about his relationship to the world can get into difficulties. He must recognize that part of his problem comes about because he makes mental pictures about the things of the world. Doing this, his gaze is diverted from the outside world to his inner world, which is filled with mental pictures. He realizes that his relationships to things begins with the pictures he himself makes and is in danger of believing that he has contacted real things. But he can come to understand that he is only looking at his mental pictures and not at the real world. He wonders if he is blind to reality. He appears to contact the world in the light of his mental pictures. He suffers from a compulsion towards a simplistic view of how he stands in the world. It is quite possible to overcome this attitude if he notices that he must also overcome this thinking. So a person can be involved with the problem of the thing itself. He can continue with thoughts that are based on a misunderstanding. For instance, many people believe they have seen something, which only exists in theory because it presents itself in a form they can imagine themselves seeing. I remarked earlier on a passenger in a train who threw open a window, because she believed that the crowded carriage was full of germs. She could not see the germs, but she could picture them to the point where she believed she saw them. People today swallow tablets that are said to contain vitamins, which they have never actually seen or tasted. In modern times intelligent people are quite ready to swallow facts or theories so long as they are related to something they *might* have seen. Perhaps people should ask themselves about what they have actually seen as opposed to what they imagine they have seen. How far are we able to live with reality, even if illusions are more pleasant?

Commentary

In considering the process of knowing the world, we face the question of our own relationship to it. We are naturally aware that we live in this world and that our destiny unfolds in it. The child starts his life in great dependence on those to whom he is entrusted through the act of birth. Today, people find it difficult to understand the process through which a baby enters this state of existence by being born. In reality, the moral impulse behind the physical event is trust in the parents, or their representatives. The community of people living on Earth make it possible for an individual to be born by responding to this trust.

At the present time, the process of producing offspring has been separated in the minds of people from the knowledge of love within the sexual act. So it comes about that to be born is an act of trust in other people who fail to realize that this is so, although the behaviour of the new-born baby continually explains it to them. The moral and physical implications are now so separated that the facts of life have become perplexities. The relationship between ourselves and the world is another question. It can be answered only by exploring what it means to be human and to find a relationship to the surrounding world. A person today is regarded as a mere onlooker at the world. The realization that if someone makes himself into an onlooker he ceases to be truly human can be awakened by asking the question that underlies many a destiny today: what am I doing here?

It is natural nowadays to accept what radio and television programmes tempt us to believe—that we are simply onlookers. If one considers the process of consciousness described in the fifth chapter of *The Philosophy of Spiritual Activity*, it reveals itself as an exercise in overcoming the illusion that we are observers in a passing world. The process depends upon realizing what thinking means in our human constitution. Everyone makes many observations in the world which he has entered through birth. They come about because the human mind, preoccupied with observing, fails to notice the other activity of the inner life, to which we attach the word thinking. The content of what one observes has become much richer. One only has to think of modern inventions, for instance, which help us move around the world so easily. In earlier times a person saw as much of the world as his legs or the energy of his horse enabled him to see. In old age Wordsworth inhabited a small house in the Lake District and, when he felt strong enough, he walked over the paths from Grasmere to Keswick. One day he discovered that the household work was done by a woman who had never seen more of the world than Grasmere itself. So he organized an outing, with a horse and cart, to the next lake down the valley. He expected her to be entranced by the adventure, but in fact what he had to face was the disappointment of the local lady when, at the end of the journey, she saw just another lake. She exclaimed that now everything—mountains, water and passing clouds—looked the same as it did at home, so limited was her world. No one today would be content with so limited a view. The landscape in this

small area in the north of England would reveal its full rich-
ness to the visitor, so wide has the area of observation become.

But the consciousness of what we observe has become a
source of error. People imagine that the understanding of
what we see is contained in the observation. We know when
we see. But there is another kind of consciousness, which
depends upon our inner life and not on what confronts us
from outside. In perceiving, we are aware of encountering a
series of unrelated impressions. They are related to each other
and to oneself by the ability to think. The impressions do not
give us thoughts, but they stimulate the mind to seek them out
and, even further, to provide understanding. This does not
come about through the ability to observe but through that
which occupies us inwardly. In fact, it overwhelms the
impression to the point that we do not know that we are
thinking. It is a further exercise on the path of questioning to
notice how much our minds owe to thinking beyond the
receiving of impressions. It is easy to observe how impressions
arise within the mind. But it is difficult to grasp the process
that goes beyond the confusion of impressions, of colour,
shape, sound and touch. This is the activity of thinking, which
unites with what is known by observation.

Within this process, it is important for a person to notice
that this inner thinking process goes beyond himself. He may
have opinions which separate him from other people, but he
has to go far beyond this by following the activity of his
thinking out into the great world, which is real and true
beyond his limited personality. If the mind only offers personal opinions, then each of us is simply an onlooker. In fact,
however, each one can become the thinker who apprehends
realities beyond himself, because he can grasp ideas bigger
than opinions. It becomes his task to live with the truth of the
greater world, if his thinking can be lifted to greater heights.
Anyone who watches his own mind can experience how he
constantly makes efforts to reach beyond his limited outlook
into the realities of existence. How can we experience that the
thinking attached to our own personal mind can reach into the

realities of the world beyond ourselves? Are thoughts more than the impression made by observation? It is proposed in this book that we should imagine thoughts to be like the flowers that blossom on a plant which has matured in its earthly development. A garden or a meadow shows that it is the nature of plants to grow and develop to a certain point, at which flowering then takes place. It is difficult for an individual to foresee how the flower will look on a certain plant, unless he has learnt by experience. Packets of seeds are nearly always sold with pictures of what can be expected. The plant achieves the revelation of itself. The reflective mind recognizes that thoughts have come into the world of matter which they will soon leave again. The mind thus transcends the limitations of perception and arrives at the knowledge of thought.

When the mind has transcended the limits of observation and arrived at thinking, it discovers that the act of knowing unites it with the realities of the universe. The mental pictures that remain behind in memory may depend on what a person thought he saw, but they are the result of bringing together thinking and observation, percept and concept. And this it is that lifts the mind beyond a mere onlooker's role into the process of reality. At this point we can begin to find an answer to the question: what am I doing here?

Hindrances to this discovery have been produced in the past by the unreal problem produced by the question of what relationship our mental pictures have to our percepts. Instead of the reality of thought, minds have become entangled in imaginary percepts that replace true thoughts. Hence it has come about that there is not enough value placed upon thinking and knowledge.

Chapter 6

INDIVIDUALITY

A question asked by philosophers is: what is a mental picture? The questioner separates himself from the things outside, but his pictures should correspond to them. But this question does not really exist. I belong to the same world as the things. In my position as a subject I am a piece of this world and through me flows a stream of world-happenings. I observe myself confined within my skin. Nevertheless, I am part of the cosmos as a whole. A further question—how do I know about the tree outside?— assumes that my bodily limits are complete. But the forces at work within my skin are similar to those outside. I am identified with the things outside in so far as I am involved in world happenings. They cause the percept of the tree. I am the one who knows the world, but I am not its creator. Therefore, through thinking I can realize what is common to both the subject—the thinker—and the object, such as the tree.

A problem is posed by the so-called physiological proof for our percepts being subjective. When I press the skin on my body I perceive pressure, just as the eye perceives light or the ear perceives sound. All are produced by mechanical processes—but are they so in reality? Matter is a series of percepts only. Certain forms of change in the object are perceived by us as movement. For instance, on a rotating surface a horse can be perceived as running if I observe the changing nature of 12 pictures one after another. The pictures produce the impression that the horse is in movement. Such a physiological fact does not help to answer the question, however.

In the same moment that I observe a percept, I start to think. A concept joins the percept. What happens then? My intuition connected with the percept remains. Later on I shall have to be aware of the connection just formed. How quickly I can do this depends on what my individual constitution allows. My percept has contacted a concept and they remain together. For instance, my concept of a lion is not formed by perceiving one, but my mental picture is. Can you have the idea of a lion without having seen one? What is changed when you have seen the animal?

A mental picture is an individualized concept. Something real is experienced when concept and percept unite. Should one observe a second thing that calls up the same concept, it is easy to recognize their connection with each other. When one encounters the same thing a second time, one meets not only the same concepts but one recognizes the object again. Mental pictures exist between percept and concept.

The sum of my mental pictures forms my experience. My ability to produce them enables me to gain from my experiences something of value. Neither the traveller who goes about thoughtlessly nor the intellectual immersed in abstract systems of thought acquires the riches of experience. Percept and concept together provide the mental picture which, in itself, is subjective.

In the act of knowing, when concept, percept and mental picture are united I have a personal relationship to the process through feeling. Human nature is twofold. In thinking we take part in a cosmic event, whereas in feeling we unite it with ourselves. Without feeling, we would become disinterested and uninvolved. Only when we connect liking and disliking with our thoughts do we become individual beings. The question arises: does feeling provide us with a richer sense of reality than thinking when we encounter the world? My feeling has only meaning for myself. Only when a feeling as a percept of myself unites with a concept can it be integrated into the cosmos. Our life is a continual interchange between an experience of the happening of the world and our individual existence. The further we rise into the common nature of thinking, where the individual becomes an example of the concept, the more we lose the character of personality. The further we descend into the depths of personal life, the more

we separate ourselves from universal existence. The true
individuality is he who reaches with his feeling into the region
of ideals. Our ability to form individual pictures gives an
individual character to our life of thought. Everyone has his
own surroundings and experiences, his place in the world from
which he perceives. He has a personal constitution by which he
directs his feeling towards his percepts, giving a distinctive
flavour to his personality. Feeling is the means by which
thoughts acquire solid life.

The human being carries his means of knowledge—observing and thinking—within himself. Other beings with other
constitutions will have their own means. Man must use what is
his: he is the human subject. The question of how similar are
the word pictures of different people belongs to metaphysical
realism. The assumption is that individual human spirits, that
is subjects, are similar—for example the ego is considered to be
a universal possession of man.

By induction, examples can be compared. This is the
modern method in philosophy. Induction once worked with
concepts, now it works with percepts. They are always open to
modification through further percepts—for example in stat-
istics and experiments. The metaphysical realist uses this
method to establish reality, but the distinction between perceiving and thinking as an exercise of knowledge is considered
to be vain even when the means of perception go beyond the
natural senses.

Commentary

If we consider that we are part of a great world, made known
to us through observation and thinking, we are then faced
with another fact, which is that we have personal experiences
that underline our separateness as individuals. To be human
means to be a combination of opposites. In our mental pictures, we are faced with memories which arise through the
process of alternating between our personalities and the ideas

belonging to the greater world. We live, in fact, in a state of contradiction. I wish to be respected as a personality, but I also have a longing for knowledge that will enable me to understand the world. I can experience both if I allow myself to swing from one opposite to another. This is not just my experience, but that of other people. I belong to the world and I belong to myself, because my mind can swing between opposites.

Everyone needs to be aware of himself as a unique character. In this sense, experience is an important factor. The individual acquires content and strength from what he has gathered from within himself. But he is in danger of being too self-possessed and therefore needs to cultivate the thought life of the world. Otherwise, his self-possession will imprison him. I can experience the tree as an object but, because I am a thinker, I am aware of myself as the subject. Nevertheless, the tree and I are part of the same world and this is clear to me in so far as I am the thinker. It is not my business to become identified with the tree—my thought life must enable me to transcend myself. Any influence that disturbs the balance of this process damages the capacity to be human. Mental pictures exist between percept and concept and become effective by their relationship to the person to whom they belong.

Someone can form a mental picture, perhaps of a lion, who has never seen one in the flesh. The actual percept—if for instance he visits a zoo—may be disappointing. He will then have to reconcile the value of his mental picture with the actual percept and will, as a consequence, have a greater experience of the lion than someone who has never seen one. On the other hand, the traveller who does not take the trouble to have percepts may gain little from his journey, because he does not allow his mental pictures to be changed. But through bringing the percept and concept together, the individual can develop what he has to offer the world through his will.

In this process the importance of feeling is encountered. This capacity of the human soul endows experiences with reality. Every thought and reaction that is real to the person has been made so by feeling. It may be sympathy, because of something that one likes and enjoys, or it may be antipathy, because of something that is annoying—through both kinds of feeling a person is connected with reality. But should neither effort nor feeling be present, boredom will set in. Boredom is a state of mind brought about by oneself, by refusing to be involved. Even in unpromising circumstances, a person can avoid sinking into this condition. A person stranded by fog on an empty railway station, as I once was myself, can be rescued by the presence of another person who is interested in something unknown to the other. That person was a pigeon fancier, who had with him a crate of pigeons training to become carriers. The interest provided by this circumstance filled the time during which the train was awaited. Pigeons have never seemed the same again to that onlooker stranded on the platform. In all the changes of daily life, therefore, a person is required to organize his feelings and welcome experience.

The life of feeling needs interest for its development. It also needs to become self-dependent. No one can insist on someone else sharing his feelings. He can try to summon up certain feelings in other people, but that can only be done by discovering how to arouse their interest. There can be no insistence on the others sharing his feelings. The life of feeling is a highly personal process, entailing the responsibilities of being an individual. At the same time one must remember that, in the adventure of thinking, it is possible to realize that we are all involved with the same universe, and must accept the swing between self-interest and interest in the world as a whole.

At the present time, self-interest has great claims on the life of the mind. We feel obliged to be ourselves, but it is possible to be so absorbed in oneself that one can become isolated. How can one find the balance between oneself and others, who are also weighed down with self-interest? How can the social life be cultivated, if one's feelings have to be treated as one's own in self-isolation. Each person can control his own feelings and therefore cultivate his interest in other people by fostering awareness of what is taking place in their feelings. As an example, those who undertake any kind of public speaking or teaching may annoy their listeners by displays of their own feelings. A speaker was once advised that, before he began, he should try to make the listeners sorry for him. He arranged to do so by carrying a pile of books, which he dropped. Several members of the audience came to his rescue and gathered up the books. As he had hoped, it was an effective start to the evening meeting. But he grew accustomed to the device and repeated it too often. It then became obvious that the books were there only to be dropped, so he was obliged to change his method. But the principle itself was convincing.

In all matters of feeling, the human soul is organized to swing from one extreme to another. A balance can be brought about if the ego becomes strong enough to control this movement. Someone who eats too much of a favourite food will find that he loses his taste for it. It is the same with music. He who craves for one kind only will ultimately be unable to stand it, because the craving has been turned into its opposite. Only someone able to control exaggeration can hope to organize a true taste that does not wear out. It is not by a person's own will that this swinging motion takes place in the feeling life—it is the nature of feeling itself to be constantly on the move. If it becomes related to the thinking mind, it can be controlled to some purpose. It is of great value in uniting thinking and willing with the person himself, so that he ceases to be merely an onlooker and becomes involved with thought and experience. Should he not be involved, he becomes an onlooker, a commentator and never a person of action. Then he can ask with some justification: what am I doing here?

Chapter 7

ARE THERE LIMITS TO KNOWLEDGE?

The whole of reality is available to us when we include ourselves in the activity of perceiving and thinking. The act of knowing overcomes the duality. Monism stands in contrast to dualism, which implies two quite separate worlds. The explanation of what happens in the one is sought in the other. It is assumed that the two regions are opposites.

Kant introduced the belief that the object of perception and the thing itself are different. It is within our spiritual organization that a particular thing can be encountered as a percept. Thinking overcomes the separateness and each percept is put into its proper place in the world whole. If our percepts are contrasted with another existence—the things themselves—there is no end to uncertainty. Everything outside percept and concept is a hypothesis; it is not an experience but a theory. The theoretical world-principle can only be upheld by something from the world of experience which connects it with its origin. The dualist maintains that the content of the concept is beyond our knowledge. It is not possible to justify bringing some elements from experience to the thing itself and call this process knowledge. For example, to contemplate the atoms of matter, which are not perceivable, and to extract scientific principles from them is not correct—they remain unreal.

The dualist has to assert that knowledge remains limited. The monist knows that what is needed to explain the encounter with a concept is already contained in it. If a person cannot find the explanation, it will be due to a weakness within himself. The requirements for gaining knowledge are there through the ego and within the ego. We handle questions but we put them to ourselves—they are not put by the world. Our questions come from ourselves because we are beings with a constitution limited in space and time to a world of concepts. I need to relate them to each other. There is no question of knowledge being limited, for what is not known today may be explained tomorrow.

The dualist carries the contrast between object and subject in our perceptions over to thought/beings outside it. Out of two factors he makes four: the object itself; the subject's percept of the object; the subject; and the concept which the percept connects with the object. The connection between object and subject is real. The subject is really influenced by the object. The process goes on outside our consciousness. An opposite effect should be made by the subject on the object, producing the perception that arises in consciousness. The dualist splits the process of knowing into two. He believes that the person can only form conceptual representations of what is objectively real. The connecting link between things and our individual spirit lies outside our consciousness and we only know a representation conceived in thought.

The dualist regards what is found in thought as too vague and he therefore wants real principles. Reality means, for the naive person, what you can touch and see. The soul is a fine material that can become visible as a ghost. The naive person wants to add to the evidence of the idea a further 'real' confirmation by the senses. The belief in revelations is like this. God must appear in bodily form. Water must really become wine. What can be known through the senses is reality. That which can be imagined in the form of sense impressions is acceptable. Tulips in the flower bed are real but not the tulip as such. It follows that only an anthropomorphic view of what is spiritual is considered to be real.

The modern scientist does the same in terms of extremely small pieces of matter. What can be conceived in thought is analogous to what is perceivable. It is inaccurate to assume that behind what cannot be perceived there are realities of the same type. This becomes metaphysical realism, in contrast to the realism of the senses, and is therefore dualistic. In fact, however, this belief can only be brought about by thinking.

The objects of perception are constantly changing. What lasts
are the forces that produce this flux. These forces are thought
of as beings with perceptible qualities. But it is wrong to accept
as real an area that is not perceptible and is only visualized
through thinking. It is clear that only thinking can establish
realities that are beyond perception. A world of percepts and a
world of concepts need to be accepted. It is useless to postulate
a world of forces, for it can only be contacted through percepts. Metaphysical realism is simply monism at another level.
Natural laws are really a conceptual expression for the relationship between certain concepts. Only in metaphysical
realism is there a real question about the limits of knowledge.

Commentary

Of what value to ourselves is our thinking? Too often in our
times it is involved with asserting our personality. In daily
affairs people encounter other personalities and have a longing to be the one who is right, who can confound their
neighbours. Every discussion, every committee meeting, every
line of argument, shows evidence of a hidden war. Just as in
sport, the question is always there: who is going to win the
match? So, in reaching decisions, the question becomes: who is
going to prevail over the others by his arguments? But this is
not the true function of thinking. To use it merely to win
arguments can only end in warfare between personalities.

The true nature of thinking is to lift the mind beyond the
personality into the area where the truth of the thought pre-
vails, where thinking minds join together purely for the sake of
truth. Beyond agreements and disagreements, thinking minds
can unite in a kind of brotherhood where the spiritual world
meets the earthly world. Thinking can rise above the level of
personal opinions into a region where truth, as the ultimate
reality, unites the ideas that represent what is personal in the
human soul. While Kant believed in something called the
thing itself, which is inaccessible to thinking, it would be more

realistic to say that we ourselves put the limit to our thinking, by deceiving ourselves into believing that we have no access to reality. Kant cast doubt upon the possibility of realities of the world becoming accessible to the human beings who live in it.

In these days it is quite possible to experience ourselves wandering about in an unmanageable state of affairs. In ordinary life we handle many things that we don't understand or know how to control. Only experts are expected to understand why our elaborate machinery does not work, or breaks down. Someone else has to be summoned to deal with the faulty vacuum cleaner, or put right the engine which has given up. Neighbours are just as helpless as we are, but it never occurs to us to reduce the equipment we live with to tools we can understand. Power and understanding do not meet in our lives. So it comes about that we are continually faced with dilemmas and our affairs are controlled by inventions we cannot cope with. We are not so much concerned with the things themselves, but with the powers that surround us and are beyond our control. The world threatens us through our ignorance.

But there is a redemption from this state of affairs. When thinking is set free from the limits of the personality, it can encounter the world beyond the human, where we become involved with superhuman questions. Being greater than we are, they challenge us to become greater than our present selves. The world may become more confusing, but if our imaginative thinking is released it can enlarge the scope of our comprehension. The problem begins with ourselves.

If we assume that our ability to think is limited by our personality, we come to a standstill. But if we are persuaded that what is real can be grasped in thought, we enter the larger universe where the eternal soul finds itself again. In the springtime we see the plants and trees coming into blossom, revealing the secret life that had been hidden during the winter. When the mind embarks upon imaginative thinking, it is a kind of springtime of the soul. Thoughts blossom because they are realities of the mind. Just as the lilac appears on the bush, or the cherry blossom on the tree, they reveal a reality hidden until that moment. True spiritual thoughts are not opinions but belong to the realities of the world. They appear in human minds because that is where they belong. Out of the universe, where the plants were united with their creator thoughts, the human being follows them into the earthly world, where his thoughts come to meet them. Human beings are not creators, but thinkers who manifest their origin in wisdom. The history of humanity is one of development. There is still more for mankind to bring forth, but in our time it is the treasure of thought to which each human mind can contribute, thus finding its place in the world and revealing its blossom as the thoughts emerge. But to realize this involves a new and further understanding of what the ability to think implies.

Creative thinking develops in us when we are willing to undertake it. What we do not comprehend now can be understood later. Thoughts are not limited, because thinking is not. It is a gift to human minds, which can blossom in thought again and again. We are not onlookers because we can come into blossom, showing the beings· of nature that of which they are truly the reflection. They have not been made by us, but they are revealed to us. Knowing is the creative process which we recognize in each other, for we all share in it.

Discovering that the mind can think for itself and be responsible for itself can make one aware that it has other capacities than those of thinking and feeling. It also has forces of will that produce action by which the world can be altered. Just as feeling comes alive in the human soul, carrying with it a sense of reality, so willing produces a stronger experience of being active in reality than thinking. But this depends upon regarding one's personal relationship to the world as being more vital than the relationship to the universe, which is produced by grasping ideas. Such experiences confine the mind to earthly realities and can deceive it about its relationship to the universe. All of us have experienced the universe as our home in the period before we were born, and we know we shall return to it at death. Life on Earth offers us opportunities to be active here because of our inner abilities—thinking, feeling and willing. A strong sense of egohood enables us to handle them on our own responsibility. In developing our abilities we come to realize that our egohood, which expresses itself in our responsibilities, is not something that exists in isolation. We can recognize the abilities emerging in other people and can find community with them in acknowledging their individual qualities. So it is that this book, *The Philosophy or Spiritual Activity*, begins with thinking as a human reality and then passes in the second half to the other reality of will which, united with feeling, makes individual action possible. In our inner nature we are responsible for these three activities—thinking, feeling and willing.

PART TWO

The Reality of Freedom

In later years, Rudolf Steiner said that he looked upon *The Philosophy of Spiritual Activity* as a Christian book. He added that the second half of the book provides a description of how a Christian today can form and control his actions. It is worth remembering that such information can help us to deal with our problems out of a Christ-informed conscience.

One follower and friend of Rudolf Steiner, Dr Walter Johannes Stein, who later became known for his work in Britain, described a conversation he had with Rudolf Steiner, who said: 'Anthroposophy is a Being, created by a deed of freedom, of free spiritual activity.' Dr Stein asked: 'What will be left of your work after thousands of years?' Steiner answered: Only *The Philosophy of Spiritual Activity*, but everything else is contained in it.'*

* From *Rudolf Steiner's Life and Work* by W.J. Stein.

Chapter 8

THE FACTORS OF LIFE

At this point it is important to look back and see how far we have come on this journey of exploration. The human being sees the world as a collection of separate things, among which he includes himself. This arrangement of the world is taken for granted and, unless we become active ourselves, it appears as a percept. When we perceive ourselves, it is one percept among many, but the sum of all other percepts we associate with ourselves. Something new is added to the picture; something appears which is not only a percept but is the effect of an activity that arises within the percept of ourselves. This inner activity reaches beyond the self. It causes the other percepts to have a relationship with each other, uniting them into a whole. Because this percept of self has a relationship to all other percepts, it results in the subject, or ego, experiencing itself as object. This mysterious activity is thinking, and what is produced are concepts and ideas. Thinking makes itself known in the percept of the self, but this self is not subjective, because it is only with the help of thinking that it turns into the subject. Thinking is the necessity in life that forms our personality. Through it we have an existence in ideas. We become aware of ourselves as thinking beings. If no other relationship to life came about, we would be beings whose life consisted wholly of producing relationships in thought between percepts. We would be entirely taken up with becoming beings who know.

It is not enough to perceive oneself as a thinking being. We also have the ability to feel. It is possible to experience the life of feeling within the personality as more real than the element of knowing. This comes about because feeling in its subjective aspect is the same as perceiving on the objective side. A naive person will maintain that all that can be perceived is real.

Feeling will therefore assure him that his own personality is real. But to this way of thinking (monism), feeling appears as less real than the concept or idea. In daily life, feeling appears like perceiving before the process of knowing. We feel ourselves as existing until, in the process of becoming, the concept of ourselves appears. Thus naive people believe that they meet their true existence in feeling. But such a person is making feeling into the means of knowing; because feeling is quite personal, he makes it into a world principle, whereas it actually only belongs to himself. Philosophy based on feeling is mystical. It has the drawback that the philosopher wants to experience what in fact he ought to know, which means that individual feeling is treated as something universal. Feeling is purely individual and is an expression of what is only a subjective experience.

The human personality has yet another quality. In thinking the ego lives in the life of the world; in feeling the person experiences the effect of the object on himself as subject. But he also lives in the activity of will. If he calls upon willing without thinking, he encounters the object of perception, and so the naive person believes that he meets a more real existence through action than he can find through thinking. Something is made to happen in the outside world. In philosophy, some thinkers believe that they have made an impression on the events of the world by the exertion of the will. It seems to them that the will they know within themselves is a true measure of reality. They make the will into a world principle, because they know it within themselves. What is important for themselves acquires the same importance for the world itself. Such beliefs are important to those who are dissatisfied with carrying into the world the ability to think. Like those who believe only in their feelings, they have only one contact with reality and that is through the percept. The truth about a human being is that he has two sources of knowledge. The one is through thinking, the other through perceiving; by their means he discovers what happens to himself through feeling and willing. Otherwise, perceiving and thinking are left standing side by side, without the knowledge that gives them both an inner reality. Mystical feeling and the philosophy of will cannot become knowledge, because then the individual is only capable of cherishing perception for itself.

There is also a way of thinking that arises when metaphysical realism becomes the object of thought. This produces assumptions of realities that are unjustified, because they are not available to perception. The mind tends to invent perceptions in areas where real knowledge can only be grasped through thinking.

Commentary

The second half of·the journey of exploration in this book begins with a consideration of what thinking really means in the spiritual life of the human mind. It reveals how prejudices from the past have tied thought too strongly to the personality. We have seen how thinking lifts the mind beyond the personality into the realities of the universe. The other capacities of feeling and willing cannot do this; they are essentially personal, while thinking can be universal. It is worth noticing that this is a fresh view of thinking, calling upon the mind of the individual to embrace realities higher than personal experience. Because thoughts are treated as personal opinions in ordinary life, great confusion exists about the distinction between thinking, feeling and willing. Nowadays, thinking is regarded as an ability each person has for himself, which should not be interfered with by others. In actual fact, the right to independent thought has never been so endangered as it is at present. Each person should be in charge of his own mind, but over and over again attempts are made to hinder the development of that which gives individuals an awareness of their own dignity.

Advertising is usually considered to be a respectable profession, even though it is devoted to persuading people to adopt certain beliefs and actions. In the days of Thomas

Carlyle, who launched a great attack on this newly-established profession, he claimed that the moral quality of people's lives could be ruined by the attempt to direct their will in certain directions without thought or discrimination. For example, when the ice-cream cart first appeared in our streets it advertised its wares with the help of music designed to awaken longing for the product. In an attempt to awaken an instinctive action in the buyer, thinking was bypassed. The music awakened the conviction that such a treat would be good for the buyer. One day it occurred to a beer advertiser that those who played in cricket or tennis matches lost some of their sharpness through alcohol. It then became the custom to reward those who had won the matches so that they could celebrate their success with the beer. The motivation was shifted, and the appeal of the product became more and more widespread. This procedure has now developed to the point where a person is asked to estimate his efforts and ability in the light of his entitlement to receive an alcoholic reward. A moral decision is called upon to promote the sale of beer.

If someone today makes a resolve to think for himself, he will find himself confronting many methods that attempt to provide him with ready-made thoughts. If he reads a newspaper, for example, he can receive many such ready-made thoughts. But by reading continually he is offered the opportunity to disagree, or think over, what is proposed in print. But there are other media which are much more capable of suppressing the opportunity of thinking for oneself, especially when they are used carelessly and in competition with what is going on in the surroundings. Anyone who turns on a radio and then undertakes another occupation, or carries on a conversation on a different subject with someone in the same room, may be unaware of how his mind is being influenced. Common opinions are spread throughout the modern world by electrical devices. Many who are proud to acquire such instruments fail to notice that they are being deprived of their own thoughts. Some people resent the interference caused by what most regard as a conventional piece of equipment. From time to time an individual may try to protect himself and his inner life by disagreeing, or by protesting. A man once came to my front door to deliver some kind of parcel. When the door was opened, he said: 'All those at home are immersed in the television and I am planting dahlias,' and with that he disappeared! A nanny from a home for old people, who had long since retired, spoke about the conversations she had with herself about the realities of life. Then she would point to her very small radio and say: 'That's not what they say in there.' She continually protested against ready-made thoughts.

Those who believe they can seek out truth by their own efforts are obliged to protect themselves against the flow of ready-made thoughts that continually obstruct them. They are often to be found seeking someone to talk to, who will allow them to express what they have discovered. In earlier ages a fierce fight was waged to protect dogma and force it on everyone. Even now, threats are used against people who pursue their own way of thinking; this is because, in spite of everything, thoughts are still found to have power. In these nervous times one dogma pursues another. Thoughts are reduced to the level of personal opinions, which only serve to protect the power of the personality. This is the final illusion about thoughts. They help one to become a person, but not to be a citizen of the universe, out of which we have all been born.

Thinking is a gift from the heavens that unites the human mind with the creative thoughts through which God has made the world. The individual is endowed with a force from outside his earthly life and he can make a place within his own being for a human response to a divine gift. But there is often a sad discrepancy between the wonder of this gift and what is made of it. When are my thoughts worthy of their wonderful origin? A respect for the divine nature of what lives within the human mind would heal much of the inner turmoil that besets people today. The question—can ˙I have thoughts worthy of my thinking?—would help people to realize that everyone has brought with him through the gate of birth a wonderful gift, passed on to him by the Angels, Archangels and all the

Company of Heaven. It is the mission of those spiritual beings in the heavens who follow Christ that concern for the gifts of the spirit should be passed on to human souls who have undertaken life on the Earth. The discovery of thinking—not of thoughts—is the inspiration allowed to us humans by God Himself, which can be discovered as we live on the Earth. The many forces of opposition have discovered ingenious ways to prevent the realization of what thinking is in the world of today. In the area of the mind, each one of us has to face temptations which are rarely recognized as such. Where can we encounter truth? Where are we supported from above against the misuse of what we discover? How can we protect the gifts of the mind against the temptations of those who would destroy the spiritual nature of man?

Chapter 9

THE IDEA OF FREEDOM

In the act of knowing, the concept of a tree is related to the percept, the connection between them being decided through thinking. The relationship between the percept and its concept is observed after the act of perceiving; the connection between the two is produced in the thing itself. Something different happens when the relationship of the individual to the world is considered. It has been shown that light falls on this relationship through observation. In this way, thinking is found to be something contained in itself. Anyone trying to explain thinking with the help of some other consideration—for instance, the physical processes in the brain, or some spiritual process apart from thinking itself—overlooks what thinking really is. The act of observing thinking leads to the direct observation of its inherent spiritual activity, real in itself. In considering thinking, that which is otherwise separated—concept and percept—is fused.

Anyone who fails to realize this is likely to experience concepts as mere shadows of what has been perceived in percepts. It can also lead to constructing a metaphysical world, based upon the pattern of the observed world. In referring to this world as the world of atoms, the world of the will or of an unconscious world of spirit, it will be overlooked that this metaphysical world is fashioned on the lines of the world of percepts. But anyone who takes seriously what thinking is will recognize that the percept is only a part of reality; the other part appears in the thought-filled experience of the percepts. Thinking will not then be regarded as a shadow of reality but as a truly existing spiritual activity. Then it can be seen that intuition is present in consciousness, that it is the experiencing of a purely spiritual content. Only through intuition can it be observed that the conscious experience of a purely spiritual content is taking place.

When this is grasped, the way is open for understanding the human organization in body and soul. While this organism cannot affect the being of thinking, it is obvious that human thinking appears to ordinary experience only in and through this organism. Nevertheless, it is not affected by it. The relationship between thinking and the human organism must be understood. In reality, when thinking takes place the organism retreats. It ceases to be active and makes a free place where thinking can appear. The reality that works in thinking has a dual effect; after the organism withdraws its own activity, it takes the place of that activity. Thinking appears in that region, so that its reflection can be found in the bodily organism. It is important not to confuse the reflection with thinking itself. If someone walks over a muddy piece of ground, his footprints are reflected there. No one is tempted to say that the footprints are produced by the forces in the ground. In the same way, if anyone observes the being of thinking, the effect on the spiritual organism will not be ascribed to thinking itself.

Another question arises. If the human organism has no part in the being of thinking, how does this affect the human being? That which occurs in the organism through thinking has nothing to do with its own being, but it affects the appearance of the ego consciousness. Within the separate being of thinking the ego itself is not to be found, only the ego consciousness. The ego is to be found within thinking. It appears there because, in consciousness, the impress of thinking is present. This should not be confused with the assumption that the ego consciousness is dependent on the bodily organism. Once it appears in thinking, it is part of the spiritual reality.

Ego consciousness rests on the human organism and out of it flow the actions of will. How, then, does an act of will take place? Two factors must be considered: the motive and the spring (or 'driving force') of action. The motive belongs to the realm of concepts; the spring of action is a factor in the organism of the will. The motive is the original force that drives the will; the spring of action belongs to the lasting character of the individual. The motive belongs to the realm of mental pictures, but they work upon the constitution of the individual according to his character. Different people are moved to different actions. An act is not only the result of a concept or a mental picture but also of the individual character of the person concerned. Each individual has in his life a certain moral, ethical tendency formed out of the content of his character. The content of my mental pictures is formed through the sum of concepts which have contacted my percepts. My ability for intuition and the area of my observations form my inner pictures, especially in contact with my feeling world. The mental picture that forms the motive provides the impetus for my will; my character decides what I do about it. It is possible to picture myself taking a walk in the next half hour—that will decide the aim of my behaviour. But this will only be effective if I am already likely to value the advantages of walking—for instance, its effect on health. We have to reckon with mental pictures and concepts that become motives and also the effect they have on the kind of character I have developed. This shows me how the moral impulses are related to the individual life.

The first step in our individual life is observation, especially through the senses. In this area we react, with or without feeling. Our drives are often aimed at satisfying our purely animal requirements. Thus the will is governed by that belonging to the lowest form of sensual life. This can be extended to the actions that operate between people, such as social convention and tact. The second sphere of human life is feeling, and emotions can be the spring of action. Seeing someone who is angry can motivate me to do something for him. This is true of other feelings, too, like shame and pride, a sense of guilt and a sense of gratitude, or feelings connected with loyalty and love.

The third step in life is thinking and forming mental pictures. They can become sources of action if aims are connected with them. Pictures of action may enter people's consciousness because similar actions have been performed before. The pictures of previous actions tend to act upon the will. For instance, I am fond of offering cups of tea to people who are in trouble. Clear thinking, without relation to certain customs, produces concepts that are the result of pure intuition. Such concepts have nothing to do with the action I took last time. The motives are produced by clear thinking. It is obvious, therefore, that when a motive arises out of intuition it will not be born out of what is customary. When a feeling works upon my mental pictures, it will take the form of what I imagine. The activity of feeling is not yet there. This part of the process may be entirely egotistical, or connected with the hope that others will benefit. It can also be connected entirely with moral principles stemming from what is customary in the family, from the society in which one lives, or the authority of church or state. In our own inner life this authority may speak with the voice of conscience. The moral life may also be decided on a higher level, by one's moral imagination. The realization of motives are therefore an expression of one's individual moral aims, whether these have been inspired by the principles of other people or by one's ability to use imagination in moral questions. The highest level of motive arises from pure thinking and practical reasoning. Only those able to grasp moral intuitions can perform truly individual actions.

Kant's principle—act so that your actions will be equally good for everyone—makes it impossible for individual impulses to be acceptable. Not what everyone would do but what is best for *me* to do is the point. Only if I can rise beyond the standpoint of the moral principle being the same for everybody can I approach individual and free action. Otherwise I am obliged to do only that which is considered right by everyone else. Each person has an individual ability for intuition and will be moved by what it tells him. The highest form of moral action is that which arises in the individual's own imagination. Only in this way can actions be morally creative.

When I perform an action, my moral impulses are connected with my love of what I wish to achieve. If I act on principle, I am simply carrying out the right ideas automatically. Only if I can act out of enthusiasm and love for the object of the action will I be free. Not that which is right for everybody will inspire me with a motive, but my love for the action itself. Only when an action arises from an intuition is it truly individual. Criminal deeds or bad deeds never come about in this way because, instead of being individual, they follow the impulses that belong to everyone. My instincts and passions do not belong to my individual purposes but to that which works in all human souls. An action that can be called free is inspired from the aims and ideals of my own self. A moral action is my action. An action born of freedom includes the moral principles that belong to everybody. The sense of duty, however, makes freedom impossible. Therefore, freedom in action arises from the ethical aims and ideals of the individual. What, then, of the life that human beings share with each other? It is generally thought that moral life depends upon an order acceptable to everyone. But in reality an awareness of the spiritual world, which gives us our intuition, leads me to the world we all share. There is something wrong about the concept of conflict between morally free persons. An action born out of love inspires respect for the will of other free people. If there were no natural impulse to find enthusiasm for the impulses of another person, this could only be brought about if individualities were united in the spirit. But in the deeper being of everyone there lives the reality of the free person. We are all bound together by this impulse. The truest form of a human being is the one that is capable of freedom.

Each individual is required to overcome the double nature reflected in his awareness of percept and concept. When he unites the two and can produce his actions out of his free spirit, then he finds himself in a form that he can recognize in others. Just as the plant unfolds its proper form as it grows, so a human being can unfold from himself the free individual that is his aim. Kant praised the sense of duty, because he believed it to be the best in human moral nature. But it is possible to take another line and find that freedom is the highest form of humanity. When I rely not upon right laws but on my moral imagination, it shows me what love really is. Moral ideals arising in individuals confer love on the moral world order. The human being is the true source of morality and the experience of it does not remain with himself but inspires the moral life in the community.

Commentary

Anyone who looks around the modern world is liable to ask: 'What am I doing here?' He then finds that the only person who can answer this question is himself. The journey from one question to another has led to the question which reveals that we ourselves are ultimately responsible for what happens in the history of mankind. We are at the centre of all its evolving.

Our relationship to technology poses a problem. Are we to be educated in spite of it, or because of it? Are we to become servants of machines, or master them so that they serve us? Will they merely save us a lot of trouble, or will they over-whelm our way of life? Are we in control, or are they? Do we destroy the Earth on which we live by relying overmuch on them? If we abandon them, do we retire into a primitive way of living? Are we progressing, or retreating? Is the news, which reaches us every day and makes us aware of the whole world, instead of just our little bit, a warning against destruction, or a confirmation of our skill?

Is there a point of reality in the modern world on which we can rely? Is our ability to ask questions carrying us into the wilderness? There is, in fact, within the human mind itself, a point of reliance, a place where the thinking mind can begin to find itself in touch with reality. I can find myself and I can also transcend myself in the reality of thinking. On the level of ordinary consciousness I make observations. In so doing, I notice that thoughts are attracted to my thinking, in a manner that enlightens the mind.

What is observed and what is thought prove to be connected by their own nature. Experience shows that any mistakes are reflected in the inner pictures. Only when thinking stops is the contact with reality endangered. But the process of bringing together percept and concept belongs to a reality of its own nature and, where the mind can rise to spiritual content, it is realized that percept and concept are the same. When a spiritual content rouses a spiritually real percept and concept, the mind becomes able to handle intuition—that is to say, a truly spiritual content is available to the thinking mind. The individual who performs acts of intuition stretches his mind beyond his individuality towards a real and objective spiritual world. At that level all individuals share contact with the same truth. Everyone who relies upon his ability for enhanced thinking can reach beyond himself to contact a greater world that can be shared with everyone who raises his ability to think with intuition.

When that which seems to be most individual, and therefore promotes the experience of being alone, is raised to a higher level of imagination, it produces intuition. A comprehension then dawns that can be shared with other minds. It opens up an objective reality on which the thinker can rely. All too often nowadays experiences shared with others are at a level that leads to argument. When each person wishes to stress his own point of view, there can be no community with other minds. If this is considered to be the level on which one finds freedom, it will prove illusory, promoting relationships that will come to expression in the biblical War of All Against All. If such thoughts and behaviour are cultivated, they will lead to reliance on authority instead of on oneself. The philosopher Kant, whose ideas have influenced modern life far more than is realized, maintained that actions that are right for me are also right for everyone. But this is no way to experience freedom. Only the moral decision of an individual can be the motive from which a free action flows. How then can such a method of turning thought into action, thinking into willing, be truly free?

This question leads to another observation—that good actions are creative and depend upon moral imagination. All good principles will then be included in that which a moral mind can picture. All that is wrong, destructive and criminal in human behaviour emerges from our common world of instincts, which each person can encounter in himself. Every good impulse involves a person freeing himself from such qualities. Human beings cease to be individuals when they allow themselves to be roused to destructive and egotistical actions. To rise above such impulses, a person needs to seek the inner freedom to act for himself out of enthusiasm for his ideals. Only at this point can the individual find community with others on the level of their ideals.

Each person can experience in his own heart that freedom is something for which he is working, that he is striving to develop it out of his own aims and ideals. No one can claim to be free, but he can strive towards freedom as the next higher expression of the human self. He can confirm his confidence in the true power of an aim that he cannot yet wholly achieve. Freedom can be developed by striving to lift himself out of the common human nature, which is the source of destructive actions. If he is able to watch this process, he can find that his whole constitution is supporting it, for his mind is related to physical processes. In one sense they affect the thinking mind; on the other hand, when thinking is raised actively towards the spiritual realities beyond oneself, the forces in the physical constitution withdraw. They allow the thinking process to engage those forces that produce consciousness. The higher part of the human soul appears in which the egohood can live and in which the awareness of the spiritual individuality within each human soul can make itself felt. The quality of egohood is there. Once it has been established, it can, with the help of the constitution, continue to be present. Its appearance depends upon achieving a relationship between soul, mind and body that allows for intuition in thought. Once this relationship between spirit, soul and body is established, the individual mind can find the moral position for its freedom. The individual can harmonize with others. The free man is born within as the reality of our human nature. He is the source of all morality and of all progress towards freedom. Each one must make a free person of himself. Only then can a true community with other people be born, through which all can help each other towards the capacity for intuition. Freedom is not loneliness, but a respect for that in others which one finds in oneself. Where people meet each other out of their instincts, strife, competition and the War of All Against All is bound to appear. Where the gift of intuition can be recognized in oneself and in others, the capacity for true egohood is confirmed.

Chapter 10

FREEDOM IN PHILOSOPHY

The ordinary naive person is one who accepts as real what his eyes can see and his hands can touch. He therefore requires for his moral life impulses that are observable to the senses. At the same time he requires an authority available to his senses, who can produce impulses of the same nature. He looks to a person wiser and more powerful than himself, or to one who recognizes a higher power from which the impulses come. He accepts his moral principles from those authorities who pronounce them within the family, the state or the church, for instance. He requires perceptible powers that can enforce his moral behaviour, but always such powers that are perceptible to him. If he discovers that he is dealing with people no wiser than himself, he tends to demand a divine Being behind them, whom he can endow with perceptible characteristics. But he expects of this Being that the content of his moral life will be expressed in perceptible form; for instance, he requires a God in a burning bush who, in a human form, walks among people who open their ears to the commands which they should carry out, or not carry out. The highest stage in the development of this naive realism comes when the moral idea appears separated from the higher Being and is perceived as an absolute force within the inner life. Once this was heard as the voice of God from outside; it later became accepted as an independent power in his own inner life and is called conscience.

But a stage has now been reached when the moral laws are accepted as the requirement of inner standards. They then stand there for themselves, but are assumed to have metaphysical being through which they exist. They resemble the forces of metaphysical realism, independent of human thinking. Standards of behaviour that become part of this metaphysical realism are believed to have their origin in a realm that is beyond what belongs to the human being. These forces appear in different guises. For the materialist, they consist in purely mechanical laws that appear to the human being as mechanical necessities which he believes himself to be connected with. Any concept of freedom is therefore an illusion. I assume that I am the creator of my actions. I might even think myself free, but all my actions would, in fact, be the effects of my bodily and physical organism. Only because we do not recognize the motives acting upon us can we have the feeling of freedom. But this feeling of freedom, arising without any conscious motive involved with it, means that our actions can never be truly free.

Another possibility is that someone will believe in a non-human, absolute power behind all appearances. Here he will seek the impulse to action through such spiritual power. He will ascribe to this power the moral principles he requires for his reason. Moral laws appear as directed by this absolute power and the human being must, with his reason, explore the advice of this absolute Being. What he perceives seems to be a reflection of a higher order. Morality is not connected with the human being but with the Being of superhuman quality, which he imagines to exist and must be obeyed. For example, in the philosophy of Eduard von Hartmann, such a Being appears to be divine and is believed to have an existence that is made up of suffering. This divine Being has created the world in order to relieve Himself of this burden.

This philosopher regards the moral development of humanity as a process intended to release the Godhead. Furthermore, he describes the Incarnation of this Godhead as portrayed in the story of the Passion of this God become flesh, and he regards the experience of morality as the assistance given to this process of suffering and release. Here the human being does not act as he wishes but out of the necessity to release God. The materialist makes the human being into an automaton as the result of mechanical forces, and the spir-

itualist can make man into the slave of the divine will. There is
no freedom in either case.

The naive believer in metaphysical realism finds no reason
for freedom, because the human being has become the
instrument of principles forced upon him. He is always the
object of another being, imposing either a mechanical or a
moral pattern upon him. Whoever is incapable of grasping the
right idea of intuition is obliged to receive his moral impulses
from outside and is, therefore, unfree. But in the monistic
outlook the idea has a reality equal to that of the percept. The
idea, however, can only express itself through the human
individuality. The impulses that come from within himself
make him free. He can only be unfree when he follows the
forces from outside. When someone speaks of another person
as unfree he must discover in the perceptible world the force
that has worked upon him. In reality, someone who thinks like
this perceives himself to be partly free and partly unfree. In the
world of percepts he perceives unfreedom, but in himself he
makes real the free spirit. Where moral laws operate, they are
the effect of the thoughts of a human being. He is not under
the pressure of a world order. He follows his own will rather
than that of a Being beyond himself. Behind the active human
being there are not the purposes of a world order strange to
himself but a world that makes real intuitive ideas for our
human purposes. The world of ideas lives in him, as an individual. What seems to be the common aim of the whole of
humanity is the coagulation of individual acts of will. Each of
us is called upon to become a free spirit in the same way that
every rosebud strives to be a rose. This is the true philosophy
of freedom in the area of conscious, moral behaviour.

Because the human being is not a finished product that can
unfold its full humanity at every stage, the problem has arisen
of whether the human being is free or unfree. He should be
regarded as a being in process of development seeking to fulfil
his aim at every point on the journey towards becoming a free
spirit. Man is not yet a free spirit, but he is led from one step to
another until the point where he finds himself as a free being.

But it should be made clear that a being under continual physical or moral pressures cannot be truly moral. He passes through the stage where instinctive, natural forces drive him from one action to another, where obedient behaviour is a necessary preparation for morality. Both these are stages from which he will be released through the free spirit. Good moral behaviour is a specific characteristic of the human being, and freedom is the human form of being moral. It is achieved because the human mind is capable of contacting a universal knowledge and having an individual experience of it.

Commentary

The question asked in this chapter is: how do the moral impulses of the human soul become active in his actions? Is he involved in the process, or does he accept it under pressure from forces outside himself? Thus the experience of being free or unfree enters the area of human behaviour. Who decides the question of morality? Who inspires the principles of a good action? Who determines an action intended to be good— myself or an authority beyond me?

We have studied the different stages through which an individual goes in his struggle with the morality of what he does. A person entirely devoted to the world of percepts, which he will most likely call facts, struggles with the world around him. He may believe that he is in need of objective guidance beyond himself. Where will he find it? How will he submit himself to laws and rules? A practical example is provided by the British Highway Code. It lays down rules in behaviour when driving a car in traffic. It gives instruction on how to deal with other people using the same road and carries penalties against those who refuse to conform. Different countries prescribe different obligations about the use of the road, laying down whether the driver should keep to the left-hand side, or the right. Obviously, the rules of the road must be acceptable to all who travel if collisions are to be avoided. How can one disagree?

Once upon a time a young woman took to driving a car through London when most of the traffic consisted of horse-drawn buses. She continued to do so during the period when cars replaced them and she often liked to speak of her experiences at that time. In her old age, she used to say that the Highway Code was 90 per cent good manners. If drivers recognized that the road must be shared with others, they would allow for the needs of those who travelled beside them. When each driver considers only himself, regulations are necessary about the manner in which one treats the other. Every driver abides by a set of regulations which would be quite unnecessary if each one was aware of those around him. Either there is consideration, or a set of rules. The latter are enforced by penalties. But if each one considered the needs of all, if he put his imagination to work, regulations and penalties would become unnecessary and a good driver would provide the pattern for those around him. He would experience himself as freely offering courtesy to others on the road. Regulations and penalties would come about by the inner choice of the drivers.

Can we decide for ourselves, as individuals, what other people need from their neighbours, or can we only deal with rules and penalties? Freedom is a matter of how the individual person solves his own problems and deals with the needs of those around him. If the ability to think is taken seriously, it produces trust between people. Order does not then depend upon law. An individual may decide for himself what kind of behaviour will create good effects in situations where his neighbours are involved. Where there is too little trust in other people, rules and regulations are the only answer. But they will never produce evidence of human freedom. The most creative actions will be those through which the individual person produces his thinking, feeling and willing out of himself.

Motives for action are individually produced, and willing is that part of the human being which directly affects the world around. A person can think for himself; the moment when thought becomes action, however, it enters the world that is shared by others. But is this the only way in which an individual makes his impression on the community? In our ability to think, we can also transcend our limitations. It may seem as if thinking only gives us our own point of view. This is only true of the limited kind of thinking that the intellect produces. There is another, greater one, where the world of ideas becomes available to those who seek objective reality. In this region all kinds of thoughts meet. We can find ourselves lifted beyond our own point of view and united in the reality of the world of ideas.

We can easily accept that the world of percepts perceived by our senses is shared, despite the fact that our impressions of it may differ. It requires development of our ability to think before we can find our way into the common world of the spirit and can experience community with other thinkers. Because of this, we lose contact with the creative abilities of our mind, through which we discover the creative spirit within. In the experience of freedom, what we have in common, what we share in creative thinking, becomes a real experience. When we know that we can think with others, our isolation as individuals is overcome. Without losing our inner freedom, we discover we can meet with other creative minds in our experience of a shared world.

In thinking we touch upon the ability of ourselves and our fellow men to create. Every action for which the motive is produced from outside injures the development of what can be created through the human spirit. Modern life is filled with obstacles to the development of inner freedom of this kind. Perhaps Thomas Carlyle was correct in attacking advertising as something that would undermine the powers of decision in people. Pictures of motives that no one has made for himself are presented in advertisements. They present aims and purposes which are thrust upon people, who should be finding them in their own thought and imagination. Even the presentation of news items exerts an influence upon one's understanding and therefore on one's sympathies. Public opinion is moulded by what is seen and heard in news items, which are so carelessly accepted today. Who takes care to preserve an impartial aptitude for judgement when it is so easy to accept outside opinions?

It is very dangerous not to preserve one's sense of responsibility when it is so ceaselessly subjected to judgements and experiences from outside. This sense of responsibility is brought about by freedom of thinking. How often is that harmed? It happens by making it easy for a person of good will to become an onlooker when he should be protecting his sense of responsibility. Only by cultivating one's inner freedom can one become valuable to the community. The people around us have so many different degrees of freedom that common understanding is made difficult. Nevertheless, no one wishes to live in this world alone, nor would this be a true part of our modern history. We are involved with each other in the development from one stage of freedom to another.

Chapter 11

THE PURPOSE OF THE WORLD AND THE PURPOSE OF LIFE

It is important to face the problem of means and ends in areas to which they do not belong. Means and ends are a particular form of consequence in the unfolding of appearances. It is present when the effect of a later event is decided by what happened earlier. This is present only in human activity. The human being produces an action for which he makes a mental picture beforehand, allowing this to decide what will be done. What comes later, that is to say the action, works with the mental picture, which is a necessary element. In this process, which is divided into cause and effect, the percept comes before the concept, which appear side by side in our consciousness. The percept of the effect can only be connected with the cause. The effect can only have a real influence on the cause by way of the concept, because the perceptual factor is not yet present. Should anyone insist that the blossom is the aim of the root, then that can only be maintained through thinking. The perceptual element of the blossom has no existence before the appearance of the root. For instance, the bulbs of a tulip are planted before the root exists. The effect of the later stage on the earlier must influence the cause. If the cause is in the concept, this is so only in human undertakings; only there can the effect be related to the cause. In the perceived process, the connection between the two cannot be found—it is only dreamt of. In subjective action, the concept of a purpose is assumed. The naive person assumes that this is also true in the affairs of nature. The human being makes the means serve the ends and, in the same manner, the realist makes the creator build the organism. This false picture of ends and means disappears only gradually. It is still usual in philosophy to ask about the purpose of the world outside and beyond itself.

Therefore the concept of means and aims outside the human sphere must be rejected. It is possible to look for natural law but not for natural ends. Only that is filled with purpose which a human being does. An individual has only the ends for which he himself is responsible. If someone asks what is the aim of a person in life, the only answer can be: that which he decides within himself. I choose myself what I intend to be. Ideas only have a purpose when a human being makes them real. One cannot speak of ideas moving through history. It is not possible to say that history is the evolution of man towards freedom, although some philosophers have said that as long as there are active impulses in nature it is foolish to deny that they have aims. The formation of an organ in the human body does not come about as the result of an idea moving towards an aim but arises from the connection with the whole, of which the organ is a part. The theory of aims cannot apply to a plan with which nature is inspired, in which for life there is no death and in development no contrasting disintegration.

Thinking in terms of means and ends produces an arrangement of percepts, making a whole. But because we assume that all percepts are arranged into a whole by laws which our thinking discovers, so the parts of the perceived whole are recognized in the members of the idea. The animal, for instance, is not influenced by an impulse moving through the air, but one which it is born with and is a natural law produced by the idea. The idea is not outside the thing but is within it. In nature there is no being subject to plans from outside; everything is originally planned from within. I invent a machine for purposes in which the parts serve the whole. The machine works according to the idea that lies behind it. The machine is therefore an object of perception, including the corresponding idea. One could say the same of the beings of nature. But one should not confuse nature's operation with that of a subjective human action. There the aim is necessary and the original impulse is a concept related to the effect. In nature, however, this process is not seen. The human concept is always related to the relationship between ends and means. Means in nature can only be deduced from percepts. Some thinkers imagine that such connections are the result of an absolute world Being realizing its aims. Others maintain that this is a hypothesis, assuming that the world also works with ends and means.

Commentary

Being human, we can observe the way we turn thought into action. Our daily lives consist largely in being concerned with this process. In our life of thought, we begin to be concerned with what we intend to do. It is the business of our capacity for thought to find aims which will enter the world as purposeful actions. All the people going down the road have thought out purposes that make it worth while going into the street and walking. 'Where am I going and what for?' is my question. But another question can be put to those whom I meet on the way: 'Where are you going and what for?' If small children are with the grown-ups, one can notice that they have different intentions from their companions. The mother may say: 'We need more bread in the kitchen.' The child may stop on the way and say: 'Here is a low wall and I must walk along it so that I develop my ability to balance.' The bread is a sideline. The mother may say: 'If I'm to wait any longer, I may miss the bread because it will all be sold.' The child may say: 'If I do not walk along this wall, I shall not develop the proper sense of balance, for which it was worthwhile coming out with you.' Both are animated by pictures that they carry in their own being. If they are turned into action, quite different aims will be revealed. The mother and the child will be aware of different aims and ways of fulfilling them.

Because the mental pictures of these actions are so different, it is easy to confuse one with the other. As the pictures turn into motives for doing, it may easily be overlooked that the pictures are quite different, although they are equally involved with finding the means for the ends and both are pressing for fulfilment. If a large puddle arises between buildings in a thunder storm, the aims and ends of the grown-ups will be to get rid of the water, whereas the ways and means of the children will be to keep it as long as possible for the pleasure of splashing. Both are forming pictures in the mind of desirable results and finding the means to bring them about. At the end of the day one should be able to ask: 'What have I done, and how did I do it? Was it worthwhile? Has the aim been fulfilled?' The questions are transformed into: 'What will be worth doing tomorrow? As the struggle for aims and means is dissolved in sleep, is my purpose unfinished?'

On a higher level, the same process is repeated on the deathbed. 'What have I done that fulfils itself? Where are the motives which have not been fulfilled and which will produce my new aims in the future? Are there pictures in my soul of further, higher aims, which will accompany me beyond death?' It is wise for the comforters to experience the questions and to support them. Everyone will die into the future, even if those around try to bring them back to the present. 'What are you talking about?' said one mother to her children. 'I am dying and it's hard work. I am forming my purposes.' The aims are present as mental pictures. The will is rousing itself for actions of fulfilment. It is not so that dying is the end of everything. There is so much present that is striving towards action, so much that is to be fulfilled.

Such mental processes are so impressive that they tend to be carried out of the personality into the world beyond oneself. An effort is therefore required to overcome the tendency to look for the same processes in the surrounding world, especially in the world of nature. Everything that is man-made— for instance, every kind of machinery—is invented for a purpose, which is fulfilled when human activity is roused. But that which applies to the sphere of human life is frequently projected into non-human activities and so become sources of error. Those who enjoy eating honey may say: 'The bees are flying through the air to look for the nectar in the flowers for the sake of making honey.' This would be so if they were human. But making the honey is part of a nature process inspiring those creatures who carry it out. That which is divided between thinking and willing in the human mind does not apply to the creatures of nature. They are born into processes of activity real to their own being. Because the capacity is within them, they continue to perform the actions. The function within and the outer process belong together; it is unnecessary for intentions to be undertaken out of inner will. Those who understand how such inner processes lead to action will not apply them to bees, cows or other creatures. It is quite in order to ask some person who is knitting: 'What are you making?' But it is incorrect to ask the world of animals and plants: 'Why are you doing this?' They are merely expressing that for which their organs were created. We can certainly question what will become of us humans if we hinder the activities of animals, insects and plants, with whom we should be living on good terms. Why are we obstructing what lives within them, preventing the unfolding of the activity through which they contribute to the world?

How can we transform what we see around us into the living thoughts through which we understand that which is different from ourselves? How can we develop the wisdom that begins in recognizing different kinds of consciousness? How can we bring about circumstances in which the human will can assist that which lives in plants and animals and can control what comes about through machinery? How can we create harmony?

Chapter 12

MORAL IMAGINATION

The path of exploration is now leading us to see that intuitions grasped by our thinking must be put into practice. He who has no concept of freedom will choose from what is available and will act according to previous experiences, depending on his own memories or on what he has been led to believe God has provided. But this is not so for someone who has experienced freedom. His resolve for action will be original. He is not moved by previous experience or by what has been ordained—his action will be carried out within the whole content of the perceived situation. The concept of each single instance will be connected with the percept—that is to say, the concept of the lion, for example, will be connected with the single lion before him. The necessary mediator between the two is the mental picture. Now the unfree mind has this mediator already provided. Motives are mental pictures in consciousness, and authority exercises its main force through such pictures. The good Christian does not act according to the teachings of Christ—he follows His good example. Rules have less value for positive action than they do for avoiding action. Laws tend to be more effective when they are forbidding something. Regulations about what one should do are usually in concrete form—for instance, sweep the street in front of your house. Concepts are often used in laws to prevent action—for instance, do not steal. They imply that there are penalties, or twinges of conscience or threat of damnation.

The individual concrete picture must be found when the impulse to action is in a generalized form. The one who thinks in freedom will always make this transition himself. Such concrete pictures require a person with imagination. The free mind, therefore, needs to develop the ability for moral imagination. This is the source of being morally productive. People who preach about moral principles are really unproductive; but moral imagination must be active in a distinct area of percepts. Human action does not produce percepts but gives a new form to the perceived world. One must always find a useful way of changing the situation—therefore a practical knowledge of the world in which one acts has to be included. Moral ideas, found with imagination, also require the skill to change the situation; this is called moral technique and is something that can be learnt. People today, however, usually prefer to find concepts in an already complete world than to summon up the imagination to visualise actions that have not yet happened. They accept moral pictures from others rather than make them themselves, and often those with moral imagination but lacking the technical skill will look for this in someone else. Others seek to make the moral life subject to laws, in the same way as they deal with problems of diet. But the comparison is false: our moral life is not the same as our physical organism. This is because our bodily organism has been presented to us already finished, whereas we must create our moral standards. These cannot be known before they have been created. The notion that we can inherit moral standards is an error, because they belong to the individual. They do not, as the laws of nature do, belong to a being simply because of its species. As a being with a moral life, I am an individual.

This view appears to contradict the theory of evolution as understood today. But this is not really so. Evolution in the organic world is understood to mean that the later organic form is more complete than the earlier one that preceded it. He who believes in the organic theory of evolution must picture to himself that there was once a time in the history of the Earth when someone could see, with his own eyes, the emergence of the reptiles from the proto-amniotes. Equally, that there could have been a Being in the Sun system, according to the original mist envisaged by Kant and Laplace, who watched himself moving in the world ether until he could find a place to stop. In spite of this, no one believing in the theory of evolution has ever proposed that he could picture a reptile before any reptile was seen. To do so, if he really thinks it through, he would have to maintain that in an earlier stage of evolution he could, from the concept of the incomplete thing, derive the concept of the complete one. Equally, in terms of moral laws, no one can foresee from an earlier form what the later one will be like, nor can a new moral idea be modelled upon a previous one. In terms of moral being, the individual produces his own content. It may be that earlier moral ideas give rise to later ones, but no one can produce new moral ideas out of those that have gone before, because they lie in the moral actions that are produced as facts. Ethical standards must first be produced in action before they can be recognized.

The ethical individualism represented here means that new moral concepts appear from moral imagination, for in every case the new versions arise in the course of real actions. It is not necessary to seek their origin in something that happened in the past—the Ten Commandments, for instance, or the life of Jesus on Earth. They come about as a result of what takes place in the human being himself, because he is the bearer of morality. Man's ethical individualism makes ethics into something real. Man must be known through observation and this will lead to discovering how he has developed, including the fact that the highest form of human action lies in freedom. What comes about through human deeds need not be under the pressure of necessity. If someone begins his actions with an intuitive idea, he will recognize that he is free. He will attain this through mental pictures, created out of moral imagination; but if motives arise that are produced in any other way, freedom comes to an end. The grounds for actions of will must be decided within oneself.

Outer pressures can prevent me carrying out an intention. They remove my freedom. A religious authority wishing to combat impure thoughts works against freedom when it strives to determine the conscience of other people. The human being is free only in so far as he can direct his will through purely spiritual intuitions himself.

Commentary

Someone who spends much of his time and energy in doing things may ask himself at the end of the day: what have I done? And if he is aware of the moral implications, he may say: what do I deserve? People rarely ask each other: what have you been thinking? Most people say: what have you been doing? It is important to reflect on how you have been doing something. What inner process has been going on between you and the world and between you and other people? If one asks oneself about the nature of freedom, which is the theme of *The Philosophy of Spiritual Activity*, the heart of the matter is reached in the question of how I have come to act and what in reality I have done.

Investigating what has been encountered in the course of the day often brings one to the point of saying: have I done the right thing? There is a great deal of enthusiasm today for training courses. Perhaps the interest in partaking in such courses arises from a fear that one does not know enough about the right thing. But the fact needs to be faced that 'the right thing' is a hindrance to freedom. Not I but other people decide on the value of my actions. This has become a very difficult problem. The right thing is always related to a way of thinking that stems from the past. Well-meaning people often refer to what they have been taught by authorities.

One of the most dramatic and controversial parables in the Gospels is the one about the Good Samaritan. It turns on a piece of wrong-doing, on thieves attacking a person travelling by himself on the highway. The simple story is really a complicated one. The traveller was on the road leading from Jerusalem to Jericho. At that time, the law and order derived from the Jewish tradition was very powerful in Jerusalem. The road, which one can still see today, goes down the mountain sides to the level on which the River Jordan joins the Dead Sea. At that time, Jericho retained the memories of Sodom and Gomorrah, which had been the neighbouring cities. It was still a place of extravagance, where law and order was not very strong.

In an age when it was prudent to travel with companions, why did the hero of this story leave Jerusalem for Jericho? And why did he go alone? It would have been quite easy at the time to say that he got what he deserved. Nowadays, a guide will still point out to visitors a building that is believed to be the hospice, or inn, to which the victim was taken. Set upon, robbed, badly injured, the victim lay by the roadside. Who helped him? The priest and the Levite—that is, one of a family of priests—passed by and abandoned the victim. Where were they going? Up to Jerusalem, or down to Jericho? The story does not say. If they were going back to the safe city, they were faced with the problem not of being hard hearted but of not knowing what was the right thing to do in a situation for which there were no instructions. The passer-by who used his imagination and sympathized with the victim was a Samaritan. He was a descendant of those colonists settled by the Assyrians in Samaria after the destruction of the Israelite kingdom in 722 BC. They knew about the law of Moses but only accepted the Pentateuch, hence there was much ill-feeling between them and the Jews. They were the wrong people, living beside the right ones. In this story the Samaritan is the one who listened with a sense of compassion. He acts out of the immediate experience of the victim's woes. He does not ask himself what is the right thing to do but appears to say: this man needs to be healed so that he can stand on his own feet again. He does not take him into his own home but to an inn, undertaking to pay for his care until he is healed.

And so the story goes on. When the victim has recovered his health and strength, he has to decide whether to go on to Jerusalem or return to Jericho. No advice is given to him; he faces his own destiny out of his own decision. The thieves had taken all his money and there is no record of this being replaced. No one offers him, in modern terms, a good home or a new job. He has to stand on his own feet and direct his own destiny, as soon as he is able. The Good Samaritan could have done so much more. There is a great puzzle in this parable, as much for what the Samaritan did not do as for what he did do. Did he leave an address so that he could be thanked? No one knows. One factor stands out clearly. The helpless man, who could so easily be accused of having brought his misfortune on himself, was restored to self-possession and to the strength to make his own decisions. Was this the right thing? Or should one say: the victim was put into the position of learning to be responsible for himself? Had he learnt from the disaster? That was his own business and we do not know. But the Samaritan seems to have said to himself: here is a poor victim, made helpless by wrongdoing. I am prepared to lift him out of his helplessness but not to decide on his destiny or show him how foolish he has been.

This is not the reaction of someone who has heeded 'the right thing' and distanced himself from the situation. It is a fine example of someone who understood the mystery of freedom, providing the opportunity for another human soul to find his motives within his own power of thought. In the earliest account of man's history on Earth, Cain answered Jehovah's question by saying of Abel: 'Am I my brother's keeper?' When human history on the Earth had been changed by the coming of Christ, the Son of God, the compassionate Samaritan found the answer, which allowed a human soul to develop his sense of responsibility for himself. The action of wrongdoers had taken away this responsibility; the compassion of the Samaritan restored it to him. But the question of what could become of him, because of the person he was, is left open.

Are we willing today to strive for the creative element within ourselves, which is freedom, or are we content to be protected by the right thing? The priest and the Levite sought protection; the Samaritan acted without it. He could hope for something new and creative arising from the heart of the victim. If we are to create the good, we need a higher kind of imagination that transcends the conventional concept of the right thing. We need to accept risk, to survive failure and to look continually towards the spiritual ideals that imagination reveals to us. The freedom which seems threatening to those who abide by the right thing is the creative element in the human soul, conferring on us the dignity of our humanity. While it takes us further on the way to becoming human, the right thing always holds us back. The adventure of freedom is what we are involved in as we become more truly human.

In one sense, the right thing deprives us of the coming stage of human evolution. In the risk that we run without it, we are discovering the future possibilities of what we humanly carry within us.

Chapter 13

THE VALUE OF LIFE

When one faces the question of the value of life, two opposing opinions are met with immediately. One says: the world is the very best that can be imagined and to live and act in it has the greatest importance; even the apparently bad elements are, from one point of view, a valuable contrast to the good. Evil can even be characterized as the absence of good.

There is another, contradictory opinion, which is that life is full of trouble and misery. Everywhere misery outweighs pleasure. Existence is a burden and non-existence would be a relief. There are well-known representatives of both opinions: in the case of optimism there are Shaftesbury and Leibnitz; for pessimism, Schopenhauer and Hartmann may be quoted. The former say: no better world could be possible than this, for God is good and only creates the best—only an unwise God could create what is less good. From this point of view, human action always tends to support what God has already made good.

On the other side, Schopenhauer believes that the impulse to creation is a blind force, that of will. The main effect of all willing can never be successful. Our life consists of dissatisfaction and suffering. But if action is given up, boredom is the result. Such pessimism provokes laziness, but the type of pessimism aimed at by Hartmann is of a different kind; it is intended to be based on experience. He wishes to find out by observing life whether pleasure or pain is the stronger force in the world. The sensible person will then estimate human happiness by experience and will find often enough that this is an illusion. The many sources of happiness will prove to be unsatisfactory. As this philosopher does not wish to deny the value of wisdom, he has to assume that the original Creator of the world has intended that pain should be accepted as having a good place in the world. So he regards pain as belonging to God, since the life of the world is identical with the life of God. An all-wise Being could only aim to produce freedom from pain, thus freeing itself from existence. Non-existence is the only possible aim of world creation. The moral human being should join with God in abolishing endless suffering. Humanity is intended to suffer from God and therefore bring release to God Himself. This is another form of pessimism.

What is the connection of this with actual experience? As examples, one can take someone who is hungry and, equally, one who is anxious to be a personal success. The first needs food, the second needs recognition from outside. Pleasure comes with the satisfaction of these longings, but the effort required cannot be called pain and one will find that the satisfaction paves the way for new longings. I can only call pain the result of longing that can never be fulfilled. Sometimes longing brings with it another kind of suffering. When a woman wishes to have a child, the satisfaction of her wish will mean more and more suffering as she deals with the problem of child raising.

In reality one would have to say that the effort of longing is, in itself, joy. But the pleasure does not come from fulfilling the aim. New problems arise from this achievement. Supposing that one's aim is not fulfilled; one can still remember with satisfaction the effort that had been made. It is unwise to assume that longing brings pleasure and disappointment pain. Illness is painful, with no longing having preceded it. One cannot call the wish not to be ill a positive impulse. The attempt to discover where pleasure and pain are is difficult to decide. What is the right means of finding the balance? Hartmann has decided that it is brought about by reason, but there is really no measurement for pleasure except by subjective feeling. Hartmann is doubtful whether a person is able to estimate the value of his inclination, so he prefers reason to decide the value of feeling.

How can an estimate of the value of feeling be composed?

Some pleasures start from a longing to experience them. Other pleasures, when looked at with reason, turn out to be illusions. Therefore, the person who wishes to strike a balance between pleasure and pain must estimate the value of the pleasure he found within himself. Sometimes the observation of oneself can show one's judgement to be faulty. An ambitious person may discover that the things he wishes to aim at are useless. He who is estimating the value of his experiences will have to strike out of the account all those pleasurable feelings that are, in reality, illusions. But this is not so simple. The ambitious person may have had genuine pleasure in his popularity and have discovered only later that it was all an illusion. But has his pleasure not been genuine? If I have received pleasure from certain experiences that I later regret, has not the pleasure still existed? Has not the thought of reason confused the issue? Will one not be faced with the question: where has the balance really been made between pleasure and pain? Reason alone has not been able to strike it. If the human being at any moment loses hope in a future pleasure, then his life is a failure. And yet, the number of people who commit suicide for this reason is comparatively small. Hartmann decided the matter in a strange way. He maintained that the necessity for carrying out the world intention can only appear to people who value devoted work. If their interest is only in the satisfaction of their own wishes, they will never reach this point. To remain devoted to one's egotism with hope means not to have realized how useless this is. That which strives for pleasure is to be found in human nature. Only those who realize how impossible this is to fulfil can grasp the higher aims of human existence.

But is it really possible to argue that the pessimist, realizing his egotistical aims to be useless, can be said to have overcome his egotism? If pleasure becomes impossible for people, then the only solution will be to destroy existence. If one believes that the bearer of the world's pain is God and that people should devote themselves to the release of God, then the suicide of the individual person would not contribute to this aim, even if God had created people with this intention. If God is present in all beings, the suicide of many would not in the least bit help Him. All these considerations assume that pleasure is the true measurement for the value of life. We should enquire if longing and pleasure are really a true measurement. Hunger, for instance, ceases when enough has been eaten. Eating destroys hunger, but it does so with the added pleasure of taste. If the eater were not hungry, he would not enjoy the meal. If, at the end of a lifetime, the result could be added up, it would never show a negative balance because there would always be more longing and hunger left. The more people there are who have hunger, the more the outcome of the balance is affected. In reality, longing is always related to needs. Therefore, satisfaction can only be estimated in connection with needs. We do not calculate the amount of pain in contrast to the longing but in relationship to the need. The mother who wishes for a child will not add up all the difficulties but will relate the satisfaction to the longing to have the child.

In real life a person only estimates his pleasure in connection with his longing. If he wishes to climb a mountain, the trouble in doing so will seem unimportant if his wish is strong enough. As long as a person can hope to reach what he is aiming at, he will go on suffering. He will not reckon that the trouble of attaining it is too great until he is doubtful about his hopes. One could say that, however painful the rest of life may be, the energy with which people strive after what is valuable will be more important than what they reject. The strength of the longing will have more effect upon my efforts in proportion to the intensity of my hopes. Human efforts depend upon the hopes of achieving their intentions. The pessimist believes that he will give up his efforts if his aims are not to be satisfied. But the moral strength of his ideals will, in fact, work against this tendency, for the individual is not really looking for happiness but for the value of the tasks he sets himself in life. The soul is naturally moral and will long for its ideals to be realized. It will be activated not by its pleasure in life but by the will in which the ideal intuition can live. Moral imagination gives the human being the strength to overcome pain and suffering. He will be the stronger when his moral imagination is active. He does not have to be directed by ethics because, when his imagination is active, he will be strengthened through his moral ideals. Such ideals are the inner content of his being. The aim of suppressing the wish for satisfaction will turn a person into a slave, because it will force him to do what he ought to do instead of following the ideals which he admires. Pessimism arises from a lack of respect for moral imagination. The individual human spirit is capable of finding the aims of his efforts in himself. If he can't do this, he is suffering from a lack of imagination. As far as his longings are concerned, his physical nature provides them. Only if there is no hope of man finding his aims in himself can he expect to find them from outside. Anyone who expects the human being to have his aims thrust upon him from outside has forgotten that he is a whole, capable of morally inspired longings. Moral behaviour rests upon the full development of what lies within human nature. There is no doubt that this is difficult to understand. People without moral imagination are willing to give great value to their instincts and believe that they should be able to express them anyhow. But those who believe that they can be mature human beings should be willing to strive for that which is produced by their higher nature. Then they will become capable of realizing the possibility of freedom, when the motive for actions are produced by moral intuitions. The mature person produces his values in himself, depending neither upon pleasure nor abstract duties. He estimates the value of life in the relationship of what has been achieved to what has been intended. He has outgrown the type of ethics that confused what he wills with what he should do. When the sense of duty decides the value of a person out of the relationship of what he should do to what he does do, he aims at standards set outside himself. The mature person becomes master of his being and decides for himself what is worth doing.

Commentary

What makes life worthwhile? The question opens up the problem of the difference between what I am and what I am aiming at. Even in its earliest years, the child has aims. If he cannot walk yet, he admires the children who can. What they can do becomes an object for him to achieve. On one occasion, I was faced with the problem of a child who found it difficult to stand and walk. This only child was given a tea party with two others who could run. When the evening came, she stood up by herself and made the attempt to walk. She had been surrounded by mechanical aids to get her on her feet, but the will to walk was only awakened by the sight of the other children. Development of skill in the early years comes largely through the opportunity to imitate more developed people. One can find by observation that the first stages in learning depend upon imitation. This is not a method that will be desirable later on, but in the first stages of life it is the most natural.

As the child develops into a grown-up, this force withdraws into the soul and becomes important in the moral life. It is foreshadowed in early childhood when older people become heroes to be admired and followed. Among my own memories, from the time when I lived in a small country town, there is the picture of an old white-haired gentleman who sat in the window of his house repairing shoes. When shoes were required in the family, I would accompany my mother on a visit to him. Such was my awe before his white hair and his skill that I could not say a word, much to my mother's puzzlement. I remember him still, my earliest hero. Looking round the modern world, I sometimes wonder where the modern child can find the experience on which his development of character will so much depend.

In the same street there was a lady, who seemed to me old, who used to say to small children: 'If at first you don't succeed, try, try and try again.' I found it a wearisome speech and my inspiration came from the shoemender. Before the child can receive instruction, he learns by example. When he has developed his own intelligence, then he is ready for another kind of teaching.

During these early years, the child begins to distinguish between what he does with other people and what he is doing himself. It becomes important to have the experience of doing it oneself. But what stimulates action is the discovery of one's own will, and the judgement about what one has done can become a very serious hindrance. The child must be allowed to see that he is doing what he set out to do. If he then says that he's not doing it well enough or that it is not what he intended, his power of judgement will develop too early and frustrate his ability to do. A very small boy, who had been handling a paint brush, once presented me with a sheet of paper with a few, faint strokes of colour that could not really be related one to the other. As I was preparing to ask him what the picture was about, he said: 'Isn't it beautiful? I did it myself'. Any further comment would have spoilt the picture for him and affected his confidence in being able to create more and more. At that stage in life, it is important to have discovered that one can work with a will of one's own.

The older child, about to embark on the adventures of adolescence, is quite happy to relate what he is good at and what he is not. A whole group of children will start on a discussion of that kind, without shame or disappointment. They are beginning to develop an estimation of results. It is no longer enough to experience what one is able to aim at and to ignore the results. At the later stage of growing up, the results are important and it is a mistake to ignore them. It is also unfortunate to restrict one's activities to those which one can easily achieve. Those who give up what they are learning because they are not good at it restrict their human abilities in later life. There may well come a time for decisions and for preparing for one's later life in which such judgements are healthy. There was once a boy who could not decide what he would do when he left school. His mother got hold of a book called *Five Hundred Careers for Boys*. For some time he came into the kitchen each evening to discuss with his mother these opportunities. Very carefully, with clever questions, she helped him to realize what the job descriptions involved and, at the end of some weeks, he could compare the pictures in the book with his judgements about his own life. He came, with their help, to see the aims that belonged to him, and they proved to be very real indications of what he was capable of achieving. He arrived, with no sense of failure, at a comprehension of the way of life he could follow while retaining his enthusiasm. One has to learn, from beginning to end, what one's aims are, and what they become when the results are judged fairly. Every person in adult life is involved with this kind of discretion.

There is a sad story by Rudyard Kipling called *The Light that Failed*. It describes a young soldier in India who makes a reasonably good job of his work and his friendship. One day he meets a girl from Europe who fascinates him. She spends her life with aims she cannot fulfil and with hopes she refuses to give up. She does not wish to marry him because he cannot share the determined pursuit of her hopes, with the result that both lives become tragedies. No one is to blame—they simply cannot adapt themselves at this stage of life to the facts that they encounter.

At each stage of our lives we have to face the question: 'What am I doing here?' So much attention is paid to achievements in the outer world, to jobs, to income and possessions, that the moment of truth, which is met at death, can be a shock. I once heard an elderly man saying to himself something like this: 'It seems so unfair that I have spent the early years of my life setting myself up with a job, a home, an income and a place in society and, at the end of my life, I shall not be able to take it with me and everything will fall away.' It was his way of facing the problem of what one can take through death and what must be abandoned. If one bears in mind the whole cycle of a human lifetime, one has to recall how much has been provided by the Angels for our descent into the world. It would be an illusion to suppose that one is a self-made man at birth. Further provision is made for grown-up life by education. At the time when one begins to call upon one's egohood, one is an aggregate of gifts that have been bestowed. Then comes the great transformation, which for modern people falls at the age of about 28. To neglect the crisis that occurs at this age can result in tragedy unless it is overcome. At this point in his lifetime the individual feels that his gifts have been withdrawn, that everything bestowed upon him by Angels and by other people has been taken away. He, or she, must be ready to rely upon themselves, even as they use the harvest of that which has been given. Were more attention paid nowadays to the nature of this crisis, more help could be given to those in distress. Those who die at this age, for no reason that others can see, are drawn back again into the life before birth because for higher reasons they cannot continue making a destiny for themselves on Earth. It would be unwise to see in this an occasion for blame, but it would greatly foster the strength for aims and ideals produced within the human soul by the powers of moral imagination if this crisis were to be understood in its own right.

From that time onwards the individual must depend upon the inner powers of his mind. He can begin to understand how he is responsible for himself, for his own decisions and aims, and how his spiritual activity can give him the means of discovering in his maturity what freedom really is. All that is described in this book can show him a new way of life, calling up his powers of courage and his faith in what he finds within himself. He should henceforth not be guided by concepts of right and wrong and devotion to 'the right thing'. In this matter, it must be observed with sadness that the many offers of training courses today do not really promote the development of self-responsibility within oneself. They often cause a dependence on the 'right thing' that hinders the power of moral imagination for directing decisions. Each one of us is gifted with imagination, which should be used for directing our own lives and our own aims. The effects of imagination can be shared, because one can also perceive pictures arising out of the imagination of another person. The courage required at the crisis of 28 should be extended into later years and needs to be observed with respect by other people. With this inner activity the fruits of an earthly life are formed which can then be offered to the Angels at the gate of death. But they will not be that which may have been admired in the course of Earth existence. Many spiritual adventures need to be undertaken today with the same sort of courage that once helped seafarers extend the earthly world beyond its known boundaries. What must it have meant for those who set sail from Europe, facing the danger that they might fall over the edge of the world? What does it mean for us today that we make individual decisions that will form our future destiny and feel that we stand alone in doing so?

Chapter 14

MYSELF AND THE GROUP

The conviction that a human being is intended to become a complete and free individuality would seem to be contradicted by the fact that he appears in this world as a member of a natural and whole genus. That is to say, each person is a member of a race, nation, folk, family, etc., is born into the male or female sex, and is active in this whole through church, state, and so on. The individual bears the general form and character natural to the community to which he belongs and he reflects his position within this community. Is individuality possible in these conditions? How can a person see himself as a whole, when he is always emerging from a whole and makes himself a member within it? The member of a whole will always recognize his characteristics and function according to the demands of the whole. A tribe within a folk is a whole, and everyone who belongs to it shares its characteristics. How the single member is constituted and how he behaves is decided by the character of the tribe; therefore the physiognomy and the behaviour of each one reflects the character of the whole.

If someone asks about the meaning of this or that characteristic in a human being, the usual answer will be that it is derived from the nature of the whole community. It explains his form of character; but the individual tends to free himself from the general character. The progressive person develops characteristics and functions that can only be explained by his own character. He uses the particular character of the group in order to express himself, so that he may form his own being. He accepts the nature of his group but gives it a form of his own. If the person is devoted to releasing himself from the character of the group, it is impossible to allow for his individual striving unless one can understand him as an individual.

The problem is most acute in relation to the sexes. It is easy for a man to see in a woman and a woman to see in a man the general character of the other sex and to overlook that which belongs to the individual. At present, in practical life, men suffer less than women in this respect. The social position of the woman is such that she is often regarded as merely expressing the character of her sex, while the man is usually allowed to follow his individual capacities and tendencies. The woman is constrained by the general character of her femininity. Arguments of this kind continue to be aired and demonstrate that the problem is not yet solved.

Anyone who judges people by the characteristics of their group only reaches the edge of the problem, for they overlook those who are beginning to follow their own way and decide for themselves. Below this level, people exist as representatives of race, folk and sex. Where freedom begins, in word, thought and action, the individual can no longer be determined by the character of his or her group. He must decide his concepts through his own intuitions and control his will by directing it to concrete aims that must be sought in his individual purposes. In this area the individual is a problem, particularly for the person who does not understand that he is dealing with someone who has left behind the typical way of thinking and behaving. When combining the concept with the percept through thinking, the observer must receive his concepts through his intuition. It will be impossible to understand a free individual if one's own concepts are mixed up with one's attitude towards him.

Only in so far as someone has made himself free from the influences of the group can he remain an individual and an individually free person. No one is wholly a member of the group and no one is wholly an individuality. But bit by bit each person must begin to free himself from the influence of the group, whether it is by overcoming animal instincts or the pressures of authority.

The person who cannot rise to such freedom remains within the organism to which he belongs through birth. He remains subject to the requirements of those around him. Ethical value can only be ascribed to human actions when they have begun with a person's own intuitions. What arises through ethical, individual intuition can be taken up into human communities. One can say that the moral life of humanity consists in the sum of moral imaginations in free individuals.

Commentary

We are all obliged in the crowded existence of modern times to follow certain customs enforced by law when we go out on to the street. The car driver realizes that he is now in personal charge of more energy than he is when he walks on his own two feet. The cyclist finds his personal energy magnified, and so he must have regard to a prescribed set of customs. Modern inventions have given the individual greater scope but they have also involved him in more prohibitions. Somewhere for each of us there is an open road, but it is hard to find.

The fascination of modern inventions results more and more in putting us under further pressures from the group. The dilemma reaches its height in a traffic jam. Everyone wants to move, but no one can do so because of the pressure produced by all the others who have the same purpose. So it is when someone is aware of the earthly circumstances that condition his place in society. He is subject to the group that determines his behaviour. But he carries within him an individuality that is independent of the pressure of the group. Through grasping the nature of this individuality he discovers his sense of responsibility, out of which he can apprehend freedom. In the development of his inner selfhood he finds that which does not depend upon the group but can contribute something to it. As an example, I recall travelling in a car in which a group of schoolboys were discussing the behaviour of the IRA and their methods of planting bombs where innocent passers-by could be hurt. Some of the boys were impressed by the ingenious methods used to this end, but from the seat at the back of the car one of them said in a loud voice: 'They are all cowards.' Thinking the matter over for himself, he had discovered his answer to the group around him.

Nowadays, there is much argument about what education really should be. It raises the question of what its aim is. The argument often becomes an end in itself. What should a class of children be like at what age? What should they know about the world around them? What skills should be practised? How much are the children to be formed by the group around them? But the true purpose of education is not what the children should be like but what they should become after childhood when they take their place in the world. It is the life of the grown-up that is the object of education. The proof of what part this or that child will play in the world only emerges when he becomes an individual. When parents ask whether a particular school is a good one, what does that mean? Surely it is a question directed towards the future—not to the group in the class but to the individual pupil who will emerge from the group with a sense of responsibility to the society in which he will lead his adult life.

There is also much confusion about the difference between training and education. In reality, training develops capacities that serve the group. These may be of a technical nature through which the common work goes more smoothly. Habitual movements that do not involve individual thinking or skill can be especially experienced in shops and super- markets, where goods are laid out on the shelves by the shop assistants. There was a time, however, when the same people could give advice about the use and quality of what they were selling. Individual interest was then an important part of the assistant's character. It is rare to meet such a quality today when everything is pre-packaged. A customer recently was shocked to experience the old method, and thereby realized what had changed. In a large store a small purchase was made—a piece of elastic designed to hold down a hat on a windy day. The customer was not sure how to attach the elastic to the hat for this purpose. When the very young assistant was asked to explain, she had to confess that she did not know. Suddenly she added a question of her own: 'How can I sell this to you, if I don't know how it works?' She disappeared for some time and finally reappeared with the head of the department. The trick of the elastic was shown to the customer, who was quite taken aback by the amount of interest shown in her simple question. As she thanked the assistant, she heard her say: 'How could I possibly sell something that I didn't understand myself? I had to ask someone else, because it's my business to learn and to know.'

Where the individual interests himself in knowledge and the consequences of what his actions will bring into the lives of other people, his individual sense of responsibility enriches the group. He no longer lives with the demands of the group only, under the pressure that training has put upon him, but can understand and think for himself, allowing the individual needs of the customer to be considered. The affair between customer and salesman becomes a real interchange between two individuals who have met in the shop, perhaps even one of the large stores of today that exert their own pressures on customers.

When the individual becomes aware of his responsibilities and discovers how he is related to the group in which he is functioning, he can contribute to the group that which comes from his separate self. He will then understand how freedom has its origin in that part of his own being that emerges from the shelter of the group. The contribution to the group is most fruitful when made by someone who experiences his intuitive thinking as an enrichment of that which he can only carry out within the group. That is to say, he does not rebel against the group for the sake of preserving his individuality but adds to the interest and welfare of the group that which his individual intuition allows him to discover.

FINAL QUESTIONS

The principles needed to explain the world are, according to the way of thinking described in *The Philosophy of Spiritual Activity*, taken from human experience. The origin of action, too, will be found by observing that part of human nature available to our knowledge, and in the experience of moral imagination. There are no abstract assumptions about the world; it reveals itself through perception and thinking. There is a unity experienced in the thinking observation which percepts bring to our notice that satisfies our thirst for knowledge. Anyone who looks for something more than this proves himself to be mistaken about the unity found through thinking, for the impulse to knowledge requires no more than this. Individuals are not separated from the world—they are part of it and are connected with the whole cosmos. We only appear separate because of our means of perception. This may convey the impression that we live with unreal percepts, that when they are approached through thinking they no longer seem like part of existence. But intuitive thinking shows the human being that he is part of the total existence of the universe. Thinking overcomes the appearance of separateness and unites our individual existence with the life of the cosmos. The knowledge of what is real, in contrast to the appearance produced by percepts, is the purpose of human thinking. Science tries to bring about a connection with the elements of reality, but it is thinking that makes a unity out of the world of our experience. Those who believe there is a kind of knowing beyond experience, try to find a second bond which is outside what we learn from experience and can only be assumed after the manner of metaphysics. The reason why we grasp with informed thinking how the world is put together is understood when one realizes that an original creative Being has fashioned the world according to logical laws.

One must not overlook the fact that thinking encloses both the subjective and objective, and that when the percept is united with the concept in thought the whole of reality is expressed. If we assume that in the concept we have to do with something quite subjective, we have not realized that the subjective content does not belong to the subject but is taken from the objective reality, for it is part of the reality that perceiving cannot reach. If the concept is not accepted as a reality, this will be because only the abstract form cast in one's own mind is considered. Even the tree that one perceives has no existence of its own separated from the concept—an abstract concept has no reality. Our spiritual organization continually tears apart the two factors of reality. One factor appears through perception, the other through intuition. When both are united we have reality. Everyone would accept the fact that we are living in reality, but we disagree about whether our process of knowing is real to us. In fact, thinking is neither subjective nor objective but twin sides of a principle that takes hold of reality. When we find the connection between percepts and ideas, we are living in reality. We do not need to look for something far away in the distance, for in the concept and the percept together we have what is real. The human being should come to realize that he is living in the world of reality and need not search for a higher form of reality that cannot be experienced. Thinking has the power to contact reality; there is no question of the mind interposing a subjective picture between people and reality.

For example, there is no such thing as many concepts of the lion appearing in individual people. The concept is the same for everyone, even though it can be affected by an individual's percepts. Thinking connects all perceived contents. The individual who has a percept of himself can connect it with many different people. He accepts a unified world of ideas in which absolute reality reveals itself. The ideal content of another person's mind is mine, too, although I do not see it until I think. In grasping with his thinking one part of the whole world of ideas it appears that an individual is distinguished from others through the content of his thinking. But if all these contents are put together, the thinking content of all human minds is grasped as a whole. This content is the thought life of God. Also, the spirituality that penetrates all human beings is the life in God. There is no vague, far-off other life at all; this is the illusion of those who believe that only this side of reality belongs to them. They do not comprehend what their thinking truly is. That which is constructed by abstract logic is only the human being transferred into another world. Schopenhauer believed in an absolute form of human will, Hartmann in the union of two abstractions in experience. In truth, the human spirit never reaches beyond the reality in which we live; there is no need to assume that we require another world. All assumptions that go beyond the world we know do not provide a better understanding of it.

We can only penetrate reality with concepts that belong to it. One does not even need percepts. It is unnecessary to look for a kind of thought that denies the spiritual reality of thinking itself. It is unnecessary to recognize ideas that regard what is beyond experience as objective. We do not need hypothetical metaphysics. In other words, we can do without abstractions. At the same time we do not need for our actions aims that are taken from a supposed world beyond the human. The human being must naturally follow what his moral imagination gives him. He does not need commands and laws brought from a hypothetical world beyond into this one; he must be dependent upon himself for his aims. His actions must not be determined by a strange and distant will outside himself, nor does he need to be directed by someone else's moral imagination—he can call upon his own. His will to act must come from his own world of ideas. To turn an idea into reality requires energy. He must discover an impulse of will before he can do anything, and this can only be found within himself. The human being is therefore the ultimate originator of his action. He is free.

Commentary

In our present century we are faced with the pertinent question of why we are here on Earth. There was a time when we were expected to believe that being human meant inhabiting an island in the universe and being surrounded by other worlds, bigger and more interesting. A meeting with a clever representative of the Anglican Church sticks in my memory. He was wondering how the idea of reincarnation could be fitted into his theology. He wanted to know why he, or anyone else, should come back again to the Earth when he might prefer some distant planet which would be more interesting for another type of existence. Once that question was often put but it has now ceased altogether.

Landings on the Moon have taken place. What was found? Conditions were discovered that would not in the least promise Earth dwellers a more exciting and pleasurable way of life. The human constitution is unsuited for conditions on the Moon, and those few who did go there wore contraptions providing for the needs of the human body in many awkward ways. A world fraught with lifelessness and the forces of death was revealed. The Earth seemed to be endowed with greater possibilities for life. There was no new paradise on the Moon that many excited people had anticipated.

Later on, through the use of more complicated mechanical devices, the conditions on other planets were investigated, thus leading to the discovery that the only place where mankind can have a physical existence is on the Earth itself. A great change of mood took place. Whereas the Earth had long been considered an unimportant member of the community of the stars, it suddenly became the only possible habitation for us human beings. If the principle of reincarnation is taken seriously, the Earth is the only place to which we could return for further lives in the physical world.

What then is the real situation of the human being living on Earth? He is often put in the position of being an onlooker.

Those who become involved in experiments, both social and scientific, begin to see themselves in this way because they are looking on at what is happening. There are many inventions which put us in this position. People used to know only what was happening in their neighbourhood; now we can learn every day what is going on all over the Earth. Newspapers have been augmented by the radio, enabling us to hear news world wide, and now television shows it in pictures. More elaborate ways of looking at what is happening at a distance are being developed. What can we do with all that is reported from afar? We become onlookers, wondering where our human consciousness and sense of ourselves really has a place.

In these circumstances the biggest problem has become that of knowing where we ourselves belong and who we are. If we ask about ourselves, we tend to feel lost in the modern world. But *The Philosophy of Spiritual Activity* begins with the question of how we are related to the world around us. It unfolds a picture of our relationship to ourselves and from there to the world. How do I have experiences? What capacities do I have for encountering the world of which I am aware? We can become conscious of our awareness, which offers us experiences of the world and opportunities for an active existence within it. What awakens in us through confronting the world as it is? The answer lies within the question. We are not mere onlookers but beings who ask questions. The world is here, we are here and we seek for knowledge. We have not made the world that we encounter, but our conscious mind gives us the task of knowing it. We can do this because of our capacity to observe what is around us and what is also to be found in our own mind. We also have the capacity that is most valuable to us—the ability to think. One could even say that we become aware of ourselves and our humanity because the activity of our minds stands between observing and thinking. I can realize that I am human because I can ask questions. I thus experience the two activities with myself between them, bringing them together so that I can begin to know. I do not need to go beyond my human self; I need to go into it to find the one who knows.

Looking with my self-awareness at what I find in the world, it becomes apparent that I also have forces of will with which I can act in the world. Through deeds of will I change the world in which I am acting. If I sit at home and decide to move a chair from one place to another, I have changed the world in a very small way. In the story of Goldilocks and the three bears, when the bears come home and find their porridge eaten and their beds slept in, they say: 'Who has been here?' They recognize that acts of will have taken place—evidence of the presence of a human being. What is the source of our actions but the human will? When thinking enters into it and produces changes of moral significance, the inner source of the action proves to be imagination. In this way we make our lives on Earth into reality and begin to create events instead of merely being onlookers.

When our minds reflect on ourselves and encounter how we are related to the world, we can discover what we need to know and what we should be doing and undertaking. One could even say the following. My future depends on expanding the use of my capacities. The world is not finished, because I move through it with ideals that are greater than what I know and can do. Discoveries really begin with my experience of myself. I do not need to imagine other worlds of experience and invention—I need to discover aims of a higher purpose which I have not yet found or created. One big illusion hampers human progress: it is that somewhere in the distance are worlds that I have still to explore, or that behind what I know there is a form of knowledge that is beyond my reach and I can only guess at. There is, however, another area that I can discover, and it begins with my own mind. For this exploration I can be inspired by aims and ideas which activate my will.

The adventure of thought that I undertake in *The Philosophy of Spiritual Activity* begins with a question and continues through other questions; it becomes a quest for that which lies within my own self. If I pose the question many modern people are capable of asking—what am I doing here?—a great adventure of discovery opens up. The means of going on this adventure are within myself, where I encounter the questions that arise in my meeting with the world. I need not be a lost soul—I can discover what it means to think in reality and to act in the world in which I live. If I begin to understand how I can think and move in freedom, I shall be able to discover the true nature of being human.